THE THREE RIFLES.

THE THREE RIFLES.

BY

STAMFORD SHERIDAN YOUNG,

Major 39th Middlesex R. V.

With a new Introduction by
W. S. Curtis

FIRST EDITION 1877
SECOND EDITION 1878
NEW EDITION 1997
The Chapter on Match Rifle Shooting
first appeared in the *Volunteer Services
Gazette* during 1876 and 1877 entitled
Hints on Match Rifle Shooting
by a Small-bore Shooter.

PUBLISHED BY
W. S. CURTIS (PUBLISHERS) LIMITED
P. O. Box 493, RHYL, DENBIGHSHIRE,
NORTH WALES, LL18 5XG
GREAT BRITAIN

THIS EDITION CELEBRATES THE SUCCESSFUL TOUR, IN MARCH 1997, OF THE GREAT BRITAIN LONG RANGE BLACK POWDER TARGET RIFLE TEAM TO SOUTH AFRICA.

Exactly one hundred years after the abandonment of the Black Powder Match Rifle by the Elcho Teams, a combined team of Black Powder Breech and Muzzle Loaders was formed by the National Rifle Association of Great Britain to revive the traditions of Wimbledon, Bisley, and Creedmoor in International Competition.

NEW INTRODUCTION © 1997 BY W. S. CURTIS

© 1997. THE TEXT HAS BEEN FRESHLY TYPESET IN TIMES NEW ROMAN BY THE PUBLISHER, RETAINING THE ORIGINAL SPELLING AND PUNCTUATION. THE ILLUSTRATIONS HAVE BEEN REDRAWN AND THE PUBLISHER RESERVES THE COPYRIGHT ON THEM AND THE NEW FORMAT. THE JACKET ILLUSTRATION MATCHES THAT OF THE ORIGINAL EDITIONS OF THE BOOK.

ISBN 0 948216 15 8

RILING BIBLIOGRAPHY NUMBER 1038

British Library Cataloguing-in-Publication Data.

A catalogue record for this book is available from the British Library.

INTRODUCTION

Major Young was typical of the type of keen Volunteer Rifleman who sprang from the great wave of enthusiasm for rifle shooting which started in 1859 with the Volunteer revival and the birth of the National Rifle Association. He made his name at first with the Enfield as a Private in the 11th Worcestershire Rifle Volunteers.

However, it was with the small bore Match Rifle in the International Long Range Elcho Shield Match between England, Scotland and Ireland at Wimbledon, that his reputation mainly rests. He took part in this match, as a member of the Irish Team, on twelve different occasions between 1873 and 1891. The conditions of the Match called for teams of eight firing fifteen shots each at 800, 900, and 1,000 yards.

From his first appearance in 1873 when he gained the top score in the winning team, to his last shoot in 1891 when his powers were waning, he always favoured the Gibbs-Metford and its Metford barrelled breechloading successors. This was despite the Irish preference for the Rigby which was initially used by the rest of the Team. In 1880 he started using the Farquharson-Metford breechloader, and although he used a Deeley-Metford for one year, the Farquharson remained his favourite until the end of the heavy black powder rifle era in 1896.

His Volunteer career commenced in the Worcestershire Rifle Volunteers, raised like so many others in 1859, but in 1875 he is shown as shooting for the London Rifle Brigade. In 1877, he had become a Major in the 39th Middlesex Rifle Volunteers who were redesignated the 21st Middlesex in 1880. The following year the 21st Middlesex were incorporated as a Volunteer Battalion of the Rifle Brigade. The 21st remained his Unit until he retired.

Stamford Young also distinguished himself in many other shooting matches and the respect in which he was held fully justified his production of this valuable handbook, not only for the benefit of his contemporaries, but also for all those who today take part in the revived sport of Long Range Black Powder Target Rifle Shooting.

W. S. Curtis
18th June 1997

THE THREE RIFLES.

BY

STAMFORD SHERIDAN YOUNG,

Major 39th Middlesex R. V.

NEW EDITION
1997

BASED ON THE
SECOND EDITION
ORIGINALLY PUBLISHED
BY
WILLIAM CLOWES AND SONS
IN 1878

PREFACE TO SECOND EDITION.

———————◇———————

In bringing out a second edition of "The Three Rifles" the author gratefully acknowledges the support accorded by the shooting public, and trusts that the present edition may be as successful as the first. The introduction of the Martini for the "First Stage Queen's," and the appearance of *Match Breech-loaders*, necessitate a few additional remarks (Chapters III. and V.), which may, perhaps, prove useful.

That portion of the work, in the first edition, relating to the Match rifles had already appeared in the pages of the *Volunteer Service Gazette*; and for the use of the admirable wood-cuts the author is indebted to the courtesy of the proprietors of that journal.

June, 1878

PREFACE TO FIRST EDITION.

————◇————

In bringing the accompanying treatise on rifle shooting before the riflemen of Great Britain, the author trusts that his endeavours to place the subject-matter in an interesting form may meet with the approval of the readers. Several pamphlets on rifle shooting have already appeared, but in none has the attempt been made to combine "the Snider, the military small-bore, and the Match rifle," nor has the history of small-arms and gunpowder been introduced; hence it is hoped that the present work, which treats of these several, may meet a want not hitherto supplied.

The author's excuse for his boldness in attempting to help even the tyro must lie in his having shot in the "Queen's Sixty," "the Twenties," and "the Eights;" and last, though certainly not least, to his good fortune in having amongst his most intimate friends the leading rifle experts of the day, whose aid, both practical and scientific, he most gratefully acknowledges.

C O N T E N T S

———◇———

THE THREE RIFLES.

CHAPTER I.

THE SNIDER.

So many pamphlets have appeared upon the management of the Snider, that little need be said regarding the successful manipulation of this weapon. Its power of dealing with the flight of its projectile will be fully discussed in the introductory paragraphs on the "Match rifle;" it is therefore only necessary to pass a few brief comments upon the handling of the rifle.

It will help the perplexed out of many a fog to accept as a *fact* that, occasionally, the Snider will utterly fail to obey the helm. There is a stage at which an experienced rifleman will arrive, when he can positively discriminate between himself, the elements, and the rifle, and nothing will sooner educate a man in this power of perception than the use of the "small-bore." There may be some who will object to this assertion, and deny that the rifle can ever be at fault. If such men will but investigate the question scientifically, their scepticism will speedily vanish.

As in Match rifle shooting, so in Snider shooting, the *wind* must be very carefully watched. Its effect on the Snider bullet is *much more* marked than on the Match rifle bullet; hence even greater vigilance must be exercised. Everything can be *overdone*, and the imagination is often a fruitful source of sorrow; the senses should therefore be carefully trained not to over-estimate. The configuration of the range should be considered in gauging the force of the wind. If a considerable dip exists between the firing point and the target, the force of the wind at the elevation of the bullet's flight over *that spot* would be greater than if such a dip did not exist. The velocity of the wind is reduced proportionately as it approaches the ground

— due to surface friction.   If then a dip of 20 feet, extending over a space of 100 yards, existed at, say, mid-distance, the bullet, while traversing that spot, would meet with an increased wind resistance, for which a somewhat greater allowance would be necessary.

Side Winds deflect the bullet laterally;   the aim consequently must be away from the bull's-eye in the direction from which the wind may be blowing.   The amount of the allowance must be regulated by the force of the breeze.

Head Winds retard the bullet in its flight;   hence the aim must be higher, which is accomplished by slightly raising the slide of the back-sight, by means of the "Vernier,"

Rear Winds, on the contrary, necessitate a lower aim, by lowering the slide.   For the explanation of the use of the Vernier, see chapter iv. p. 39.

Light.— There has existed for some time among Volunteers a popular superstition that the apparent target, under the influence of refraction, has a rise or drop giving a maximum variation of several feet.

In a work published in 1864, † the observed variation was stated to be four feet at 450 yards, and corresponding allowances in sighting were recommended. This delusion was neatly dissipated by the professional experience of a gentleman, who observed: " I was formerly one of Brunel's assistants, and when we started from a 'bench mark' to make a circuit of levels for canal and railway purposes extending over fifty miles, if, on bringing back the circuit to the starting point, the total error of level exceeded *three inches*, our papers were rejected as valueless.   How could such accuracy be insisted on if an error of *four feet* were possible in a single observation ?"

No one will deny that in rifle shooting variations in the elevation arise from decided changes in the light, but these are entirely due to the amount of foresight taken in aiming varying in proportion as the eye is helped or retarded in focusing the sights of the rifle, and also to the " blur " produced by strong sunlight.   Smoked or blue glass in spectacles will tend to overcome such difficulties.

† *NOTES ON RIFLE SHOOTING by Captain H. W. Heaton, 40th Lancashire R.V.*

Sights.— The slide, if reversed, can, to a moderate extent, be used as a wind-gauge, but the uprights are so close that, if more than three feet at 600 yards be necessary, aiming off for the additional quantity must be resorted to. The aim may be taken *outside* the uprights for allowances of 16 or 17 feet at 600 yards, but some difficulty and danger attaches to this. It is always safer to try and find some " spot " to aim at, and abandon the extremes of the wind-gauge dodge. Canting the rifle will give considerable lateral allowance without very materially lowering the elevation, but its application requires such skill, that it may well be regarded as dangerous.

In bad lights it is sometimes of assistance to aim, not at the bull's eye, nor on a line with it, but at the top edge of the target. Again, when targets, as at Altcar and Wimbledon, are tolerably near each other, occasionally the bull's eye or edge of an adjoining target may be made use of when aiming off many feet. Should the distance be two or three feet too much, it may be corrected by taking the windgauge on the opposite side to counteract the excess. For example, the targets are 16 feet apart from edge to edge ; the centres of the bull's-eyes then would be (on a second class target) 22 feet apart ; a right wind requiring 16 feet allowance at 600 yards prevails. How can the adjacent target be utilized ? It is clear that, as the bull's-eyes are 22 feet apart, the edge of each target is 19 feet distant from the bull's-eye of the other, *i.e.* three feet more than is required for aiming off to the *right*. Well, the aim may still be taken at the left edge of the right-hand target, despite its being 19 feet away instead of 16 feet, by taking off three feet on the bar by aiming on the left of the centre platina line, practically by aiming, so as to point the muzzle three feet to the left of the object. The 19 feet would thus be reduced to 16 feet, the necessary amount, and the advantage of having a definite spot to aim at be retained. Such make-shifts prove of great value sometimes.

Every expert has some particular modification of his own regarding the best method of using the sights. The writer prefers the following, which very possibly, many others also practise :—

At 200 yards the **V** of the back-sight should cut the *shoulders of the block* of the foresight, the tip of the "barley-corn" being placed under the bull's-eye, or wherever the aim may be.   This also applies at the longer ranges if the **V** of the slide be used.

By cutting the shoulders of the *block* in the **V**,   the amount of the foresight taken in aiming is less liable to vary than if a full or fine sight with the "barley-corn" alone be taken.   In bad lights this system is pre-eminently successful.

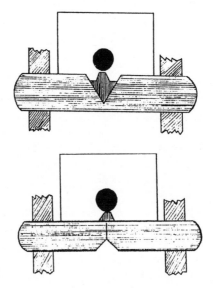

If the slide be reversed and the "knife-edge" used, the edge of the block of the foresight should be *just* visible over the "knife-edge," and the tip of the "barley-corn" placed, as before, just under the bull's-eye, or wherever the aim may be.

The difference in elevation between the bar and **V** is generally about $^{7}/_{100}$ in favour of the bar.   Some slides have deeper or shallower **V**'s than others, in which cases the amounts would vary accordingly; but as the *first* change from **V** to bar, or *vice versâ*, should only be made in *practice*, $^{7}/_{100}$ is near enough to show where the trial shots strike.

16

During very dry and hot weather, the fouling soon forms into a hard dry crust, which materially interferes with accurate results. Under such circumstances it is desirable to blow down the barrel from muzzle to breech, after having removed the fired cartridge and closed the action; this should be done immediately before loading to fire again, else the moisture set up by the condensing of the breath will have been dissipated during the long delay that sometimes occurs between two shots. When the sun is piping hot the fouling becomes very serious, as even blowing down does but little good. The only hope then is to clean out between ranges, and whenever permissible. Fire slowly, and give the barrel a chance of cooling between the shots.

Cleaning.— For range purposes, the brush with rag attached on a string with a leaden weight answers admirably. It is easily carried, and if properly used saves the muzzle the friction of the cleaning rod. The leaden weight should be inserted at the breech, and allowed to gravitate down the barrel out of the muzzle; push the brush into the chamber, and draw it and the rag slowly down, until they pass the muzzle. By keeping the rifle inverted, all the fouling will drop out at the muzzle. One or two sweeps generally suffice. When the rag and brush become soiled, the former should be renewed and the latter washed in benzoline and well dried. Where a rod is used let it be a *wooden* one, and be careful to keep it as much as possible in the centre of the barrel; even the friction of the wood will wear the muzzle. Common petroleum, also called "kerosene," "crystal oil," etc., is as good as any other lubricant and rust resister.

A gas flame makes a fine velvety, temporary black for the sights. For other "blacks," see pp. 62, 63, and 67.

Sight Protectors.— Of these there are many, and personal taste must dictate; the simpler the better. Those with corks are apt to absorb moisture and rust the muzzle.

Cartridges.— Luck governs one's fate ! All that can be done by way of precaution is to examine the nose of the bullet, and observe that it be not much indented. Also shake the cartridge close to the ear, in the hope that, if there be but a half charge of powder, the rattling together of the grains of the powder may reveal the defect. Some riflemen push the bullets down as far as they will go, by placing the nose of the bullet on the thigh and the palm of the hand on the base of the cartridge, and then pressing. This also would probably prove the means of detecting any gross error in the quantity of the powder. The process is rather a strain on the muscles, which is somewhat against its adoption.

Sucking the Bullet.— A great many good shots are guilty of this little fad. Its value is uncertain. It can do no harm, even if it be not productive of good.

Barrel.— Iron or Steel ? Not long since steel barrels were the rage, and those using them were almost regarded as stealing a march upon their poorer comrades, who could not afford to purchase private-made Sniders. The writer, however, has always preferred iron barrels. Three steel barrels, all by different makers, failed in his hands to give as good results as iron barrels; and this opinion is now confirmed by the majority of our leading shots returning to their first loves, iron barrels !

Mr. Turner, of Fisher Street, Birmingham, manufactures excellent Sniders. The writer, and some fifty friends who use Mr. T.'s Sniders, have had every reason to be thoroughly satisfied. Mr. T. is at present working up a military small-bore breech-loader, which from all accounts, seems likely to be a reliable weapon. His double sporting rifles have, on several occasions, won the *first* prizes in "Northern India Rifle Association" matches. Such successes confirm the conviction that he is a thoroughly competent and skilled rifle manufacturer.

General Hints and Cautions for the Tyro.— Do not be too despondent if your first essay in public be a lamentable break-down. Some of the best Snider shots in Great Britain very often are subject to the same humiliation.

Avoid asking every friend and casual acquaintance what his score may be, what elevation he has used, and what allowance for wind. With the best of intentions he may mislead you. Learn rather to trust to your own judgment, and the sooner you boldly strike out for yourself, the sooner will independence be your happy lot !

Do not be guided too readily by a single shot. A cautious policy must be adopted. Keep a sharp look out upon the targets where "good men and true" may happen to be shooting, and note their results. A change in the wind, otherwise unperceived, may sometimes be thus detected in time.

Be generous in your feelings towards your brother competitors. Never deliberately mislead any one. If self-interest should dictate not giving the "straight tip" to your adversary when he inquires where you "held," don't put him off the scent; rather boldly say you prefer keeping your counsel. Indeed, it is always well to avoid to avoid giving advice; for, no matter how honest it may be, its worth is measured, not by its merit, but by the results it may yield the individual acting upon it. If he should succeed he will probably hardly thank you; whereas, if he be unlucky, everyone is informed that "So-and-so" told him all wrong !

Help to keep up the high tone of rifle shooting by avoiding in yourself, and denouncing in others, any attempt at being "too sharp for the Executive."

CHAPTER II.

MILITARY SMALL - BORE.

THE issue of the Martini-Henry to H.M.'s "Regulars" clearly points to the abolition of the "big-bore" and the substitution of the "small-bore." How soon the change may affect the Volunteers it is not possible to predict, but any reflecting mind cannot fail to recognize the danger that would exist in the event of *two sizes* of ammunition being required in actual warfare. In the bustle and confusion of a sharply contested engagement, it would by no means be an unlikely mishap to find that the two supplies were despatched to the wrong troops — the Sniders offered Martini ammunition, and the Martinis silenced by being served with Snider cartridges. Moreover, it would demoralize the best troops in the world to be crushed by the superior power of the enemy's weapons. To be raked by the foe's bullets at 1000 or 1200 yards, without being able to return the compliment, would naturally shake the nerves of the finest soldiers. Hence it does not appear unreasonable to assume that, so soon as any real danger should threaten our shores, a determined effort would be made to arm the Auxiliaries with the same rifles as used by the Regulars. It must therefore be most advantageous that the Volunteers should be encouraged to familiarize themselves with the military small-bore, and learn to shoot at the longer ranges.

The National Rifle Association deserves the nation's gratitude for thus taking the initiative in training the manhood of Great Britain to the use of the military small-bore, and also for giving an impetus to the production of a superior military breech-loader, by throwing open the competitions to all manufacturers whose rifles are constructed upon certain fundamental military principles.

It is always a disagreeable task to cry "stinking fish," much more so when the national reputation is implicated. Naturally every Briton likes to feel that his armies are the best *armed* in the world, and that they are possessed of the finest rifles extant. But, when actual facts do not confirm this happy thought, it becomes a duty to look matters honestly in the face, and endeavour to ascertain whether the mental deductions have been fairly arrived at, or are but the visions of some painfully delusive nightmare.

It has been stated by many celebrated rifle experts, at Wimbledon and elsewhere, that the Martini is nothing more nor less than "*a miserable malformation.*" This anathema by no means proves that it is *inferior* to the Snider, for few would attempt to deny its superiority at the longer ranges. The point at issue is that the mechanism was so faulty, alterations, involving a considerable outlay of public money, have had to be freely introduced to make the action at all reliable, and after all this *patching up*, the arm is still *much inferior* to some already in the hands of the shooting public.

It would occupy many pages to treat the subject fairly and liberally and critically, and such an infliction would probably bore the general reader.

We have the reports of the colonels of the various regiments to whom the Martini has been issued, a perusal of which will show how conflicting are their opinions, though it is only just to state that, on the whole, the military verdict has been in favour of the Martini-Henry. The solace derived from this fact is, however, rudely disturbed when we find the Martini most completely whipped out of the field, in the Wimbledon contests, by almost every other small-bore, and we then rightly recall to mind the fact that the colonels who reported favourably upon the Martini were only called upon to discriminate between it and the Snider. But its superiority to its old predecessor, after all, really means but little.

At Wimbledon "*the Sixty,*" in the second stage for "the Queen's," use the Martini-Henry. "The Sixty," be it remembered, are the so-called *sixty best marksmen* in the Volunteer force, and mighty men must they therefore be ! A reference to the annual reports of the "National Rifle Association," however, will show that the majority of these unfortunates are handed down to posterity as *rank duffers*: men who can hardly hit the targets ! Some so hopelessly bad that they did not even attempt to "fight it out," but modestly retired *in toto.*

All this is very unsatisfactory. It tends to prove two things — one, that the Martini-Henry is, more or less, a treacherous weapon; the other, that it is impossible to learn the tricks of this tricky rifle in the limited practice available at Wimbledon, which however, in future, will be obviated by the adoption of the Martini-Henry for both stages of "the Queen's," whereby competitors can familiarize themselves with their rifles over the various ranges before coming to Wimbledon.

Another spectacle is also significant. The Martini-Henry seldom creeps into the prize list at the *long ranges*, despite the luck that always attaches to numbers.

The test of a rifle may justly be assumed to lie in its performance at, say, 1000 yards. A reference to the results of the competitions for the "Duke of Cambridge's" prize at 1000 yards, culled from the reports of the N.R.A., shows that in

1871 the prize was won by Metford barrel with W.R. action.

1872	"	"	"	ditto	ditto.
1873	"	"	"	Henry.	
1874	"	"	"	Metford with Farquharson action.	
1875	"	"	"	ditto	ditto.
1876	"	"	"	ditto	ditto.
1877	"	"	"	ditto	ditto.

Thus, it will be seen that the Metford barrel has, *six* out of *seven* times, choked off the Martini-Henry and all other rival military small-bores.

The writer, by preference, uses a "Metford-Farquharson," and has no hesitation in pronouncing it to be a thoroughly reliable rifle. Its performances have occasionally, when a soft, mellow light has prevailed, quite equalled the shooting of the *Match* rifle. It is hard to conceive a more perfect military arm. The barrel, the action, the cartridge, are all alike unique.

Rival manufacturers may possibly resent this recommendation of a particular weapon, but these papers are compiled for the benefit of the shooting public, and not for the profits of the trade. The one aim and object of this little treatise is to endeavour to help the *beginner*, and to try and foster the manly and useful pastime of rifle shooting, both practical and scientific.

Maker of Metford-Farquharson.— Mr. Gibbs, 29, Corn Street, Bristol, in whose hands Mr. Metford has, for many years, placed the manufacture of his rifle. Every barrel is carefully examined and supervised by Mr. Metford, as his "stamps" on each rifle testify. (See also pp. 26 and 35).

Breech Action.— The barrel is fitted to Farquharson's action; the sliding block enables the cleaning rod to be entered at the *breech*, thereby doing away with the danger of *wearing the muzzle* by the rod's friction. The interior of the barrel, too, can be readily examined.

Cartridge.— Solid drawn brass cases, capable of standing almost any amount of rough usage; the cost of which but slightly exceeds that of the bottle-nosed Martini cartridge, and the difference between the two, when loaded as "a *service cartridge*," cannot fail to strike the most obtuse and bigoted of partisans. The Martini ammunition would be utterly disabled by the treatment the Metford-Farquharson cartridges could endure without the least injury. The soldier's ammunition ought, undoubtedly, to be so constructed as to bear *rough handling.*

Mr. Gibbs sells cartridges loaded according to Mr. Metford's directions, but as some men prefer loading their cases, the process is best conducted somewhat thus: Procure a board an inch or two in thickness, and, say, 9 × 14 inches. Drill 50 holes in this, slightly *larger* than the *base* of the cartridge, and about two-thirds the depth of the thickness of the wood. The cases, as soon as filled with powder, should be placed in this board, which prevents them being knocked over before the powder is secured by the *wad.*

Examine each case at the entry (mouth) to see that the "burr" has been entirely removed; if not, it must be pared off with the paring tool supplied by Mr. Gibbs, otherwise the papering round the bullet will probably be rivelled back, which would be destructive to good results.

The *charge* varies from 70 to 80 grains (75 grains may be regarded as about the best for general purposes, with the 480 grain bullet); and, as the only object in loading one's own cartridges is to insure uniform accuracy, the powder should be carefully weighed to at least ¼ of a grain.

After weighing the charge, pour it into the cartridge-case, and stand the case in one of the holes of the board already described, and so on until the whole 50 (or less) are filled with powder. Next pick out one of the cases (it is best to work from right to left, beginning at the bottom), and place the "trunk" (supplied by Mr. Gibbs) upon it; put a waxed wad in and push it home, quite square, with the proper tool, but do not *crush* the powder; then insert a bullet and push it "home" also. Treat each case in the same way. Unquestionably a good deal of labour is involved in preparing one's own cartridges, and as Mr. Gibbs endeavours to issue uniformly reliable ammunition, the simplest way by far is to purchase from him.

Cleaning Fired Cases.— As the same case can be used four or five times before showing any signs of being "crippled," it may be well to describe how to treat them.

As soon as the day's work is over, stand 10 or 20 fired cases at a time up on end, fill with boiling water, then treat another batch in the same way; having done so, return to the first lot, and with a tooth-brush, cut down to fit, briskly scour out each case separately; shake up the fluid and empty into some vessel. Have a supply of hot water at hand in another basin, dip the treated case in, half fill it, place the forefinger on the mouth, and shake up the water inside; empty into the vessel containing the soiled water, and then drop the case into a third vessel containing boiling water. To treat 50 fired cases so will occupy about 20 minutes. When the 50 cases have been transferred to the last-named vessel, pour off the hot water, and quickly place each case, *mouth downwards*, into a stand bored with 50 holes just large enough to permit the cases to enter as far as the "swell." A common duster, placed under the inverted cases, so as just to be in *contact*, will absorb all drops of water that may cling to the mouth, and should be removed in about an hour. Next day the exploded cap should be knocked out with the "punch" supplied for this purpose.

It sometimes happens that the cases, from contact with the dirty water, get a darkish blue colour. This can be got rid of by washing them in common vinegar, and then plunging in boiling water and drying; but the discolouration is in no way deleterious.

A mark ought to be made on the rim of each case every time it is used, to show how often it has been fired. If there be any signs of cracking anywhere, reject the case.

Re-sizing.— The explosion of the powder enlarges the cases somewhat, for which reason they must be *swaged*, to cause them to fit with ease. Put the case, muzzle first, into the swage, and tap home; then gently knock it out.

Re-capping.— Place a cap on the cap-chamber and press home with the tool made for this purpose. Never, on any account, attempt to *re-cap* or *swage* a *loaded* case. Loss of life or limb might result.

After use, a few of the cases may be found a little too long; reject such, as they are not worth the trouble of cutting down. That they have become slightly elongated will be ascertained by not being able to push them home into the chamber of the rifle.

If fired cases are corked up immediately they are ejected out of the rifle, they will keep uncleaned a few weeks without harm; but otherwise they corrode, unless treated as already described.

Management.— The rules which govern Snider shooting, in a great measure, also apply to the military small-bore; the principal difference being that the latter has a much wider back sight, on the slide of which are drawn three fine platina lines. The centre line is supposed to be "dead on," *i.e.* when no side allowance is necessary. The line to the right will give a lateral allowance of 12 feet to the right at 1000 yards, or, roughly, a *full* foot for every 100 yards. The line to the left will give a corresponding allowance to the left, provided the rifle be dead set, *i.e.* the slight natural drift to the right taken off.

The use of the Vernier is hardly necessary with the Metford-Farquharson. On one leg of the back-sight leaf the scale is cut in 100 yards; on the other, in degrees and five-minute spaces. The eye can readily subdivide the five-minute spaces. The angles are made to agree with those used with the Match rifle; small-bore shots, therefore, have but to apply the scales of their Match rifles.

The pull-off of the trigger is exceedingly pleasant and very regular.

Cleaning out.— During the dry weather which often prevails at Wimbledon, it is generally well to clean out between ranges, though the rifle will shoot as well as any other rifle also in a dirty state. Whenever it may be required to clean out, first open the breech action; lay a piece of flannel, or swan's-down calico, two inches square, on the entry of the chamber;

25

place the jag of the cleaning rod in the centre, and push steadily from breech to muzzle, until the cloth falls out at the muzzle.

Gently withdraw the rod (a wooden one). The barrel will probably be clean; if not, another piece of cloth will complete the operation. When the fouling is very hard, it may be necessary to moisten the cloth with saliva. After the day's shooting is over, clean out, pass an oiled cloth up and down two or three times, oil the action. The difference between cleaning a Martini-Henry and the Metford-Farquharson is *very marked.*

To remove the Action.— 1. Cock the lock with the lever, unscrew the key-pin, and withdraw it.

2. Take hold of the lever, and pull out the internal lock; clean and oil it.

To put the Lock into its Place again.— Cock the lock with the lever, and put the breech-block in a little way; when this has been done, the small end of the lock-plate must be hooked in, after which all may be pushed home together. Put in the key-pin, and screw home.

Messrs. Westley Richards, of Birmingham, have lately entered into arrangements with Mr. Metford to apply his principles of rifling to the Deeley-Edge action, and are now manufacturing military and other rifles equal to any in the market.

CHAPTER III.

MARTINI - HENRY.

THE adoption of the Martini-Henry for the first stage "Queen's," renders necessary a few remarks on the management of this weapon. The principles which govern the successful use of the Snider equally apply to the Martini; therefore, those who have already mastered the Snider will find no difficulty in handling the Martini, the shooting of which will be found much more reliable than the Snider, especially when winds of variable strengths prevail.

The back-sight being considerably wider than that on the Snider, the bar can be used with greater facility as a wind-gauge. The centre platina line is intended for "dead on" at all distances, *i.e.* if the rifle be properly adjusted, which can best be ascertained by firing over the course on a calm day. The line on the right, as the eye looks towards the target, is intended to be used when wind from the right necessitates an allowance in that direction, and may be roughly computed to give 14 inches for every 100 yards; *e.g.* if the foresight be placed over the platina line on the right, and the aim be then taken at the "bull's-eye" at 500 yards, the bullet should strike about three feet clear of the right edge of the target, or, in other words, would give a lateral value of six feet. If, therefore, the force of a right wind were such as to require six feet allowance at 500 yards, the foresight should be placed over the right platina line, and the aim be taken at the "bull." The line on the left yields similar values, the necessary corrections being made to counteract any known bias of the rifle to carry to either side.

It is impossible to give any hard and fast laws for either the elevations or lateral values. These differ considerably, owing to slight variations in the rifles themselves, but more particularly to the idiosyncrasies of individuals.

The rifleman, of course, must bear in mind that the further he goes back from the target, the greater the effect of the wind pressure on the bullet, and that it is according to the distance he must gauge the necessary allowance.

The rise between distances in all good rifles should be progressive, by, say, one-hundredth of an inch, and having ascertained the rise from any one distance, the quantities for other distances are readily calculated. The average rise in the Martini from 500 to 600 yards is $^{12}/_{100}$ (.12); therefore, between 600 and 700 it should be $^{13}/_{100}$ (.13), and between 700 and 800 yards $^{14}/_{100}$ (.14), and so on. These differentials should be added to the previous range to obtain the elevation of the next 100 yards further back, so :—

Distance.	Elevation.	Differential.
500	·15	
600	·27 (15 + 12)	·12
700	·40 (27 + 13)	·13
800	·54 (40 + 14)	·14
900	·69 (54 + 15)	·15
1000	·85 (69 + 16)	·16

From this formula the rifleman can deduce his own elevations, which probably would somewhat vary from the above.

The "pull-off" of the Martini has been immensely improved, and it is not now subject to those harassing variations it once displayed. The fault is that it is too much over the minimum of six pounds. A practical rifle maker, who has experience in this particular branch, should be employed if any alteration in the "pull-off" be required, for though the construction of the action is not very intricate, the amateur had better not attempt lightening the "pull."

An indicator on the right side of the breech action shows when the rifle is at full cock, and it is always so when this indicator points towards the screw on which the pulling-block hinges. The tyro must be cautious, and never attempt to "ease springs" by trying to *hold the indicator* while pressing the trigger — a severe nip of the fingers would be the result.

Accidents have been reported; and one Martini-Henry has actually burst, to the writer's knowledge, owing to the "jag" supplied with each rifle having been left in the barrel while in the act of firing. If these must be used, they should on no account be kept *in the barrel*, but always be carried separately. The old familiar brush, attached to a loaded string, is the best cleaner for range purposes. The thorough cleaning necessary at the end of a day's shooting is best done leisurely at home, where the "jag" had better be left.

The present Wimbledon rules admit of colouring matter being applied to the sights. The peculiarity of one's visionary powers will best determine which is most clear, and at the same time the least distressing to focus over and over again. Probably a red foresight and black bar, or *vice versâ*, would prove most satisfactory. A little chrome blended with vermilion makes an excellent red.

The issue of the Martini will develop a taste for long-range shooting, and it is possible that many will soon turn their attention to the study of the more accurate weapons with which the "Elcho" is shot, and by this means new life may be instilled into a pastime at present threatened with decay. For though Match rifle shooting may be "fancy shooting," its tendencies are all in the right direction towards accuracy; and by cultivating this desire we keep our senses on the *qui vive* for advance and improvement, and thereby indirectly benefit the *soldier's rifle.*

CHAPTER IV.

MATCH RIFLE SHOOTING — MUZZLE - LOADER.

THERE are so many veteran small-bore experts in the United Kingdom that the writer approaches the subject with much diffidence, and trusts that those who are already deeply versed in the intricate *minutiæ* of this science will pardon him if he fails either to adduce anything new to them, or omits some dodges they may already know.

The primary object of these papers is rather to initiate the tyro, and awaken a more general interest in Match rifle shooting, than to attempt any scientific dissertation.

There are, however, some scientific facts connected with this branch of rifle shooting which should be more generally known and understood, and these will be treated of in everyday parlance, that all may be able to understand the principle.

It is to be regretted that Match rifle shooting is not more popular than it is. Very few *new* names appear, while, alas ! too many old and familiar ones disappear. Time, that ruthless enemy of mankind, spares not even the rifleman, and so, year by year, the numbers gradually lessen, threatening eventually to dwindle away entirely. If the effort to awaken a fresh interest in this most perfect of the branches of rifle practice be productive of any fruit, the writer will feel amply repaid. He trusts to the generosity of his readers to accept, under any circumstances, "the will for the deed."

Before entering upon the more practical parts of the subject — those relating to the details of manipulation, choice of weapon, etc. — it may not be amiss to review rifle shooting generally somewhat in the light of a science, that the differences in rifles may the more readily be appreciated.

The Snider (gas-pipe, as it is somewhat contemptuously termed) unquestionably is the arm best known to and understood by volunteers; hence it will be desirable to commence with its consideration, and lead up from it to the claims of the Match rifle.

Every year the Wimbledon meeting certifies to the really magnificent *holding* of the Volunteers of Great Britain. At 200 and 500 yards hardly a

MATCH RIFLE SHOOTING.

Snider competition is concluded without the "highest possible" score being registered, and from this fact many a conclusion is drawn. The competitor who has just made all bull's-eyes with his Snider experiences, in the height of his exultation, a feeling almost bordering upon contempt, as he passes the "small-bore" man shooting at the same distance, and failing to do equally well. The mental deduction in this instance, though a very natural one, is not sound.

The extreme accuracy of the Match rifle demands much more perfect holding than the Snider, for with it there can be no "lucky shots. " Where the muzzle points at the instant of explosion thither will the bullet speed, wind allowances, of course, being taken into consideration; whereas it is not always so with the Snider, where the rifle sometimes corrects the error of aim. But dismissing this as of no weight in the argument, the question of accuracy may be definitively settled by firing a series of shots, when the error will manifest itself.

To argue from a more scientific point, it may be well to compare the Match rifle and Snider thus: the Snider rotates its bullet about 200 times per second, while the Match rifle spins its projectile somewhat more than *five* times as rapidly ! It does not require much acquaintance with science to comprehend that the gyratory differences must be enormously in favour of the Match rifle, and that where the slowly spinning Snider bullet will get deflected from its true course, the highly stable Match rifle bullet will be unaffected. The gyroscope beautifully illustrates this law of dynamics. It may, on a humble scale, be practically demonstrated by procuring two humming tops of the same size; start one at a low rate of velocity and the other at about five times that rate, at the same moment strike each top a smart blow with a light rod. The slowly spinning one will stagger and never recover its equilibrium, whereas the other, with the higher speed, will almost immediately resume the perpendicular, and "go to sleep," as it is popularly termed.

As the base of the projectile leaves the muzzle of the rifle, the gases behind which impelled it up the barrel are, necessarily, capable of travelling at a greater speed than the bullet; consequently, at this moment, these elastic agents rush past the bullet, and if its stability (gyroscopic action) be not very great, it receives a slight deflection according to whichever side may offer the greatest resistance to the impact of the gases. That this is really the case with the Snider may be practically tested by firing a score or two of shots at 200 yards at a thin sheet of lead, say four feet square. On examining the bullet-holes carefully, it will be found that many are more like *ovals* than *circles*, thereby proving that the point of the bullet was not perfectly true, but had a bias in a given direction. The same experiment with the small-bore reveals no such defects.

It is not a very difficult matter to ascertain the rate at which the bullets rotate as they leave the muzzle of the rifle. Given the initial muzzle velocity which is obtained by firing at a "ballistic pendulum," and divide the same by the pitch of the rifling, the result will be the gyratory speed — *e.g.* the Snider's initial velocity is 1265 feet per second, the pitch of the rifling one turn in 6·5 feet; therefore, 1265 divided by 6·5 equals 194·6 for spin of bullet per second. The initial velocity of the Match rifle (Metford's) is 1400 feet per second, the pitch one turn in 17 inches — $\therefore$ $1400 \div {}^{17}/_{12} = 1400 \times {}^{12}/_{17} = {}^{16800}/_{17} = 988\cdot2$ for spin of bullet per second.

If the Snider cartridge be examined, it will be found that there is no packing (wad) between the powder and the bullet to minimize the tendency of the gases, on the instant of ignition, to escape past the bullet, before the expansion has thoroughly taken place. Should this occur, "fire cut" (as it is technically termed) ensues, and the shot must of necessity, if the "fire cut" be heavy, be a wild one; while last, though not least, the *soft* lead sets up such a cruel friction that no really reliable results can ever be reckoned upon for a certainty.

If some such decided defects did not exist, we should not so often witness the strange spectacle of men making a string of bull's-eyes, and then suddenly missing the target altogether without being able to account for it. The wonder rather is how men are lucky enough to register full scores.

With all its failures and drawbacks, the old Snider is by no means a despicable weapon, and if a few small improvements in the cartridge were permissible, its shooting could be much improved; but when contrasted with the Match rifle, it is, of course, outdistanced on all points.

MATCH RIFLE SHOOTING.

Accepting, therefore, the fact that the Match rifle is incontestably vastly superior to the Snider, the question suggests itself,　Why is it not more generally patronized ?　Amongst the hundreds of first-class Snider shots, how is it there is not the desire for a weapon that will do them more credit ? It is hard to say.　The principal reason must be that Match rifle shooting is not sufficiently understood, and that it is clothed with a halo of false light by the uninitiated, which most effectually deters men from patronizing it.　To try and remove some of this misconception is the object of this treatise.

The first cost of a small-bore and its apparatus, perhaps, has also something to do with the apparent lukewarm feeling upon the subject.　The paucity, too, of the prizes open to this class of rifle tends, in a great measure, to limit the numbers, and lastly, the erroneous belief that a novice has no chance against the experienced *habitués* of Wimbledon.

Every man who can use the Snider effectively cannot fail to do well with the Match rifle.　It there be the desire to excel, accompanied by a steady perseverance, success must inevitably follow.　No one who has experienced the charm of handling an accurate weapon will ever regret having been induced to purchase a small-bore.　Many are the bitter disappointments experienced by those who use Sniders.　Unaccountable shots in critical matches !　Who has not been driven to the depths of despair by such ? These agonies of mind are unknown among small-bore men.　Deliberate errors and gross misjudgement, of course, often dash the brightest hopes to the ground; but the rifle itself never plays false.　Treat it fairly, and it will do more than the man behind can command.

No doubt the number of the competitions open to the Match rifle is exceedingly small, and very possibly this may be another reason why so few new men turn their attention to this class of shooting; but it may be taken for granted that, if the number of competitors increased at all sensibly, the N.R.A. would not be behindhand at giving prizes.

The cost of the Match rifle and apparatus may be put down at about 25*l*. The expense of practice is not much in excess of that with the Snider, for less suffices to train one.　Considering the pleasure of such practice, and the chances of success in competitions,　the first outlay is not excessive.　Very probably the rifle will have won more than its value ere the expiration of the *first* season.

There are several manufacturers of Match rifles, all, more or less, very good; but before naming any of them, it may not be uninteresting briefly to review the circumstances which led to the present revolution in both rifling and bullets. The old theory was that the rifling should be *deep*, and the lead the *softest* that could be procured. Upon this dogma all makers apparently were agreed. Sir J. Whitworth somewhat diverged from the "good old" beaten track, when he introduced his hexagonal bore and mechanically fitting bullet, but the difficulties in fouling were so insuperable that his system gradually died a natural death. While these experiments were being conducted in the outside world, Mr. Metford, C.E., whose tastes led him to apply his engineering and mechanical knowledge to the construction of small-arms, was busy elaborating certain convictions of his own regarding the true principles of rifling, etc., and while other makers were wedded to the deep grooves and *softest* lead, he was experimenting with shallow grooves and *hardened* lead. Like everything novel, his suggestion met with disapprobation; but as "the proof of the pudding lies in the eating," the advantages of his system were soon so self evident that gradually not only was all opposition withdrawn, but his principles were adopted by every maker of any repute. The consequence is that nearly all Match rifles are now constructed very much alike. Small variations in the nature and depth of the grooves are so paltry, that it is undesirable to waste time over a description of each. One marked difference, though not yet generally captured, is Mr. Metford's formula for "a gathering spiral," based upon certain geometrical laws, whereby the tendency to strip, being uniform, is reduced to its minimum. The "gathering spiral," moreover, necessitates the *shearing* of the paper petticoat round the bullet, which absolutely insures its leaving the bullet *at the muzzle* — a most important consideration. The law which should govern the rotation of a bullet must be that the growth of the rotating movement should be exactly proportional to the growth of the linear movement of the bullet, by which means the tortional force will be uniform throughout the discharge.

MATCH RIFLE SHOOTING.

Amongst the principal makers may be named Mr. Gibbs, of Bristol, and Messrs. Westley Richards, of Birmingham (who make the Metford rifle, and it may not be amiss to state that every barrel is carefully tested by Mr. Metford himself prior to issue — a guarantee not to be over-estimated); Mr. Rigby, of Dublin; Mr. Ingram, of Glasgow; and Mr. Henry, of Edinburgh. All four are patronized by riflemen. A reference to the N.R.A. report for 1875 shows that in the International Match for the Elcho Shield, out of the twenty-four competitors, twelve used "Metford's," eight used "Rigby's," three used "Ingram's," and one used a "Henry." If the general statistics were consulted, it would be found that the Metford ranked as "first favourite," but as it is not intended to recommend any special maker, each reader must determine for himself what maker to employ.

It is important to get a rifle thoroughly adapted to one's capability. A man with a long arm and considerable reach can handle a long rifle, *i.e.* one 36 inches in the barrel, and the usual 14½ inches stock; while those of shorter stature must judge for themselves. The short barrel yields a lower rate of bullet velocity; but the loss is so trifling, that if a greater comfort in "holding" should result, there need be no scruple in ordering, say, a barrel 32 inches in length, with a stock about 13¾ to 14 inches. Comfort is unquestionably an important consideration.

Another feature to be considered in the build of the rifle is the formation of the barrel, *i.e.* whether it should taper towards the muzzle, or be uniformly thick. Modern fancy has inclined to the former, but the writer strongly holds with the latter by preference. A light muzzle is much more *sensitive* than a heavy one, and what would seem most desirable would be to have a barrel that, from its construction and distribution of weight, would *swing slowly*. The heavy muzzle undoubtedly has this desideratum. The chief difficulty in rifle shooting is to hold on to the bull's-eye; therefore every arrangement in the weapon which tends to steadiness is a step in the right direction.

As all exterior finish adds very considerably to the cost of the outfit, it is not imperative to have any engraving. The rifle shoots equally well in humble attire.

THE THREE RIFLES.

Sights.— Of these there is an immense variety; they all fit on to a movable wind-gauge, to enable the aim to be taken invariably at the bull's-eye. The divisions, as a rule, represent hundredths of an inch, and divisions of two minutes on Mr. Metford's scale. A hundredth of an inch may be computed to give a value of an inch for every hundred yards, a "minute" yielding the same result. Amongst the principal are —

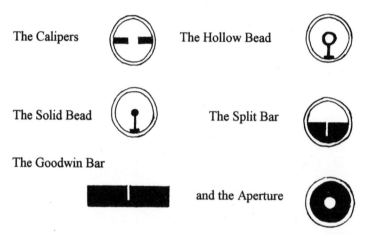

The Calipers   The Hollow Bead

The Solid Bead   The Split Bar

The Goodwin Bar

and the Aperture

In the choice and use of any of these sights, very much depends upon personal fancy. They are all used, and fine results are obtained by different men from each. The calipers, perhaps, are the greatest favourites, and should be used thus —

the bull's-eye being pinched between the calipers. Steadiness is tested by observing whether the bull's-eye is stabbed by either of the points of the caliper. It is desirable to have this sight as *wide as possible*.

The hollow bead is used by getting the bull's-eye *inside* the circle, thus -

When true in the centre, the aim is correct.

The solid bead is generally useful in very bad lights, when the bull's-eye is almost an indiscernible grey. It is then centred on the target, and treated as if it represented the bull's-eye. The eye is sufficiently keen and accurate to determine where the true centre of the target is. Of course perfect results can not be obtained with this sight, but as it is only intended for use when other and better sights are useless, it is well to have one for emergencies. The following diagram represents its application :—

The "split bar" and the "Goodwin bar" are used alike, the knife edge being placed beneath the bull's-eye, and the split or platina line used to determine the line of direction, thus —

 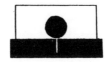

THE THREE RIFLES.

The aperture should be used thus — in fact, like the hollow bead :—

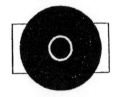

It has the disadvantage of obscuring the target, and thereby increasing the risk of firing at the *wrong target*.

The *Back-sight*, called the orthoptic, is graduated into inches and hundredths of an inch, or into degrees and minutes. A hundredth of an inch and a minute may be taken as representing an inch for every hundred yards, thus : Supposing the sight be set for 600 yards at 1° 12' (one degree and 12 minutes) ; if raised to 1° 13', the increase of the one minute should cause the bullet to strike six inches higher than the previous shot; at 1000 yards, a minute, in like manner, should represent 10 inches on the target. These values are proved to be correct by practical experience, but as it might interest some to know the scientific formula by which the result at any given distance may be obtained, it may prove useful to give the process in detail. Assume the distance to be 200 yards. Then 200 yards will be the radius of the circle, the diameter of which will be the radius multiplied by two (200 × 2), which will equal 400. To ascertain the circumference, multiply the diameter (400) by 3·1416 — which gives 1256·64 yards; this reduced to inches, 1256·64 × 3 × 12 = 45,239·04. Now, every circle contains in its circumference 21,600 minutes of angle (360° × 60' = 21,600'). Divide the number of inches in the circumference of the 200 yards' radius circle, viz. 45,239·04, by 21,600, the number of minutes in *every circle*, and the result will be 2·0948 inches ($^{45,239·04}/_{21,600}$ = 2·0948), the value found by practice to be correct. The process at 1000 yards will yield — 1000 × 2 = 2000 yards, or diameter of circle, which multiplied by 3·1416 will yield 6283·2 yards as the circumference (2000 × 3·1416 = 6283·2). This reduced to inches represents 226,195·2 (6283·2 × 3 × 12 = 226,195·2). Divide the *inches* by the number of *minutes* in every circle's circumference, and the result will be 10·47 inches ($^{226195}/_{21600}$=10·47); or, for practical purposes, 10 inches.

The calculations are *facts* as applied to all angle-taking instruments, whether it be a sextant, transit instrument, or rifle scale.

The scale is worked on the same dodge as the little elevator termed "*Vernier*," and with which Snider shots are so familiar. The principle of this cunning device is easily explained, and has been adopted with a view to facilitate the reading.

A given distance, A B, is divided into, say, *four* spaces, each representing a certain quantity, say *five*-hundredths of an inch. The sum then of the four divisions must necessarily be 20-hundredths.

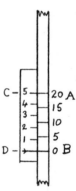

On a sliding piece of metal, alongside the upright limb, another scale is cut on a distance C D, equal to A B, but the spaces are *five* in number instead of *four*, each of which must represent $^1/_5$ of C D, or four-hundredths — thus ($^1/_5 \times ^{20}/_1 = 4$). The divisions on A B being equal to 5, and those on C D being equal to 4, it is self-evident that the difference between them is *one*. In this example the values are in hundredths of an inch, the difference one therefore represents one-hundredth of an inch; consequently if the second line, marked 1 on C D, were raised till it coincided with the line marked 5 on the main limb A B, the increase would be *one*-hundredth of an inch and so on.

The scale could also be cut to represent other values than hundredths.

Upon a screw passing down the centre of the orthoptic is attached the "saucer" — a hollow cup of metal made dead black, and perforated with a small hole, varying in size from ·03 to ·08. The first is much too small, and strains the eye too much. It is well to have two saucers — one ·05, the other ·07 — for ordinary and bad lights. The worse the light, the more reason for the use of a larger hole to look through. It is a good plan to attach an india-rubber cup to the saucer, for the double purpose of affording more shade, and for protection, in case the orthoptic should fly backwards upon the jar of the recoil. The eye should be brought as close as possible to the saucer to get the largest possible field of vision, which, of course, is contained in a *circle*. In the *middle* of this circle *centre the foresight* and align it on the target, using the foresight as already explained. As the orthoptic is liable to be slightly pressed forward by the rim of the firer's hat, it is a safeguard to attach a strong rubber band to the "small" of the stock, just behind the "pistol handle." Round this band twist a piece of copper wire, and allow the two ends to project, forming slight crooks. Insert a crook round each leg of the orthoptic, and the strain from the band, now in tension, will hold the orthoptic in position. As oil destroys all "rubbers," it is well to carry two or three spare bands to renew when necessary.

In the more expensive rifles the back-sight is kept in position by a spring, when the india-rubber band is unnecessary.

As the aim has to be taken through a small aperture, it is impossible to know whether the rifle is bedded properly in the shoulder, so as to have the sights upright. A spirit level, attached to the barrel immediately under the block of the foresight, or upon the foresight itself, enables the firer to align his rifle properly every time. After a very little practice the eye will instinctively focus the spirit level and foresight at the same moment.

Spirit bubbles attached to the sight itself, travelling with it where wind allowance is necessary, are exceedingly convenient, always being immediately under the sight, and therefore in the true line of vision; but there are some very serious drawbacks, the most fatal being that, from the constant jar at every discharge, the fittings get displaced, a very slight alteration on either side causing the marksman to *cant* his rifle unconsciously, and so lose direction. The error is so gradual in its increase that it may assume alarming proportions before being discovered, and cause much undesirable perplexity. It does not follow that the shooting will necessarily be ruined, because the experience between each shot enables the corresponding correction to be made, but if the owner of a rifle undergoing such variations be unaware of the cause, he will be considerably fogged to find his wind allowance enormously different from that of others, and possibly after some bad score be led unjustly to condemn his rifle; the patent fact of its wind allowance differences being a prominent proof in his estimation, whereas the whole secret would lie in the imperceptible (to the eye) displacement of the "travelling spirit level." For this reason a spirit level attached to the barrel is preferable, though not quite so easy to manage when a heavy gale necessitates a considerable allowance from either side.

Should the recoil seem excessive, one of Silver's anti-recoil heel-plates, or an ordinary india-rubber shoe-pad, will effectually protect the shoulder without in any way affecting the accuracy of the shot.

A small box, termed a "carrier," is an essential luxury. There are many varieties. The more compact the better; one that will contain fifty or sixty bottles, the sights, bullets, etc., is sufficiently large.

A pair of apothecary's scales that will weigh to one-eighth of a grain is a *sine quâ non*, as each charge should be weighed to at least one-fourth of a grain; success depends upon care and accuracy.

To recapitulate. The outfit should consist of 1 Match rifle with its false muzzle; 1 cleaning rod, jag, screw, etc.; 1 loading rod; 1 sight case, containing the orthoptic, 2 saucers, 3 or 4 foresights, 2 spare nipples, nipple-key and turnscrew combined; 1 spirit level; 1 carrier, with oil-bottle, etc.; 1 pair of scales and small tin funnel; 1 scoring book; 1 rifle waterproof cover.

Powder.— The best is Curtis and Harvey's No. 5 or No. 6. It is generally well to mix three or four of the 1 lb. Canisters, and then put the lot back again, so as to insure uniform density. Powders made at different dates vary somewhat in density, and for this reason the mixing is recommended. If 5 lb. canisters be used, this trouble is avoided. Always keep the powder in a dry place, because, if exposed to damp, it absorbs moisture and loses strength.

It is necessary that the powder should be quick burning to give the static bullet the required blow to expand it into the grooves, and so hermetically seal the gases. If No. 10 (a very large grain powder) be used, the bullet will hardly have a trace of rifling on it, and the shooting be bad to a degree. It is often asserted that the powder burns all the way up the barrel. This is entirely a popular delusion. The whole of the charge is consumed before the bullet has moved two inches. Experiments have satisfactorily proved this in small-arms, and common sense supports the conclusion.

41

THE THREE RIFLES.

If the powder burnt slowly all the way up the barrel, why should the breech end always be made so much stronger than the muzzle ? Again, if the barrel is cut down and down by lengths of six inches until very little is left, the speed of the bullet, if the popular theory be true, should be proportional to the consumption of the charge; whereas it is not so, the reduction in speed being proportional to the reduction of the barrel, on the assumption that the *entire* charge is consumed — *e.g.* if 36 in. barrel, with 90 grains, yields a certain muzzle velocity, 18 in. barrel will yield a velocity less only so far as regards the loss in the length of the *barrel*; the powder being still taken as *all* consumed. Moreover, the powder chamber shows by far the most considerable fouling, indicating where the gases were generated. Many other proofs could be adduced.

The Charge.— This must vary according to individual caprice — from 75 to 100 grains — but though the speed is increased nearly as the square roots of the weights of charges, it does not seem desirable to use massive quantities. The flatter trajectory with the larger quantities is obtained at great personal discomfort. The muzzle disturbance, and the general shaking up of the firer's frame, tend, in a long match, to prove destructive. It is worth noticing that the finest results are generally obtained with charges of 90 grains or thereabouts. The Americans, it is true, use much heavier charges than that recommended, but the American powder is weaker than Curtis and Harvey's, and requires a larger quantity to produce the same volume of gases. This probably explains the difference in the weights of charges.

The False Muzzle.— The object of this most admirable contrivance is to do away with all wear and tear of the real muzzle of the rifle; the last inch of a rifle is about the most important inch in the whole barrel, and should be treated with the utmost care and consideration. No loading or cleaning should ever be attempted unless the "false" muzzle be on. On the other hand, it is very necessary to remove it every time before firing, as if kept on it not only utterly spoils the result of the shot, but is blown away, and not always easily found again. To avoid this danger of forgetting to remove it, it should be tied, by the string which is affixed to it, to the "carrier," or the button-hole of the coat.

Wads.— These are apt, after being kept for a while, to get dry, and should then be saturated with *pure* "sperm" or "neat's-foot" oil. The inferior kinds of sperm are of a pale yellowish tinge of colour, while that which is really fit for use should resemble brown sherry. Allow the wads to soak for twenty-four hours, and then drain off the oil by placing the mass of wads in a glass funnel. As the oil deteriorates, it is undesirable to keep too large a stock of wads.

Cleaning.— Though the Match rifle shoots just as well after several hundred rounds have been fired from it, it is very necessary to clean out at the end of each day's work. The fouling in the barrel very soon deliquesces, and as soon as this occurs the moisture begins to set up rust, very little of which is fatal. The oiled wad, no doubt, removes nearly the whole of the fouling, carrying it down to the powder chamber; some men, therefore, after the day's practice, squib off a small charge, and load with powder and *two* wads only. However, as the trouble of cleaning is comparatively slight, it is better to clean out at the end of each day's shooting. As soon as the last shot has been fired, saturate a piece of flannel, or any fine woollen material, with ordinary "petroleum" or "kerosene" oil, and pass it down the barrel into the powder chamber; leave it there with the rod until next morning, by which time all the fouling will have adhered to the flannel, and will be drawn out with it. Then take a fresh piece of flannel, saturate it with the same fluid, pass it up and down the barrel, reverse it, and repeat the operation. If the rifle is to be used immediately, sweep out the barrel with a piece of "swan's-down calico," or any fine rag, so as to remove all trace of the "kerosene." Pour a little "sperm oil" on a fresh piece of rag, slightly lubricate the barrel by gently passing it up and down once or twice; the rifle will then be ready for action. The object of mopping out all the kerosene is that, being a highly inflammable material, it is consumed during the discharge of the first shot, and tends somewhat to increase the fouling. The sperm oil therefore should be used, if possible. But, on the other hand, if it be intended to put the rifle by for some time, the kerosene should be allowed to remain, and the rod left in the barrel. After the lapse of a few days the rod should be drawn up and down twice. The interval between these slight acts of attention may be

43

increased, as the danger of rust decreases with each fresh lubrication of the barrel. There are many cleaning fluids sold under different names, but the "kerosene" is much the cheapest, and answers very well. The sights should also be rubbed with an oiled rag after being used. After the rifle has been lying by for a long time without being used, it is desirable to fire ten or fifteen shots with bullet before entering any competition, as the oil which is used to prevent rusting is apt to form a thin skin or scale on the inside of the barrel, and it requires a dozen shots to thoroughly remove all this and bring the rifle to its proper condition — a day or two before the match answers very well. Once freely in use, i.e. if used once week, there is no need for this precaution. Benzoline, a rabid enemy of oily matter, will speedily remove any clogged oil; but as it is highly inflammable, it should be used with caution.

The test of the barrel being in perfect condition is that it should look a *dead black* inside the muzzle; if it has a grey appearance, rust has been at work, and on dry days the results will generally prove unsatisfactory.   One night's rusting is more fatal to the barrel than half a dozen year's shooting. No delicate barrel will stand such treatment and give uniformly good results. If after several thousands of shots have been fired there should occur occasional unaccountable "ricochets," the chances are the last quarter of an inch of the barrel has worn the *thousandth* of an inch, due principally to the false muzzle having become loose from wear, when, in cleaning, some of the rod's friction has attacked the real muzzle.   However, this mischief does not necessitate the purchase of a new rifle.   If the barrel be taken to its maker, and a quarter of an inch cut off, the worn part will be removed and the shooting be as good as ever.

The *lock* is a very important part, and in rainy weather is liable to become "wood-bound," due to the wet working in under the trigger. Precautions are of little avail.   It is best to remove the lock and clean it, after any prolonged exposure to bad weather, otherwise the "pull-off" will vary and become absolutely dangerous.

Bullets.— These vary slightly in weight, but the differences should not be sufficiently marked to produce any ill effects. Variations up to 22 grains have been experimented with at 1000 yards, the results being much alike.

MATCH RIFLE SHOOTING.

There happens to be, for moderate differences of weights in bullets, a compensating action, which especially exhibits itself at the long ranges; however, if greater confidence be gained by weighing the bullets, there can be no objection. Differences of three or four grains may be passed as *perfectly* safe. *Tight* bullets, which require some pounding to get them "home," should be rejected; but such bullets can be readily made to pass down nicely by rolling them between two smooth boards — one roll generally suffices. A loose bullet, *i.e.* one that will almost drop to the breech, will give a better angle than one which requires several pounds pressure to drive it "home." It is important to notice that the bullets be not badly rusted *i.e.* the paper petticoats glued to the metal by chemical action due to *damp*. The lead then assumes a dulled, pitted appearance, and the paper petticoat will be found adhering too tightly to the metal; such bullets should be rejected.

Loose bullets, *i.e.* those that almost drop to the breech, may be made to fit properly by giving them one turn in their paper petticoats.

Loading.— Having fitted the barrel into the stock, point the muzzle to the ground, and snap a couple of caps to clear out the nipple chamber. So many serious accidents have resulted through the reprehensible trick of pointing the muzzle at other people while snapping caps, the writer warns the beginner never to fall into this dangerous habit. Go up invariably to the "blowing-off-pit," and snap into it; after snapping, half cock the rifle, remove the old exploded cap, and blow down the barrel to see if the passage be clear; if it be, put on the false muzzle and proceed to load. Pour down the powder, observing that the whole of the charge is emptied out of the glass bottle; lay two wads on the mouth of the false muzzle, and press home with a steady sweep. Remove the false muzzle and squib into the pit. Should the rifle fail to go off after two or three caps have been fired, unscrew the nipple and work some powder into the chamber, then screw back the nipple, taking care to observe that no powder remains in the thread of the screw, nor in the nipple seat below the screw. Fire a cap or two, and the rifle will explode.

Many men fire a bullet into the pit, instead of merely squibbing with two wads as recommended, but the writer always avoids doing so for two reasons — firstly, that very frequently the "blowing-off-pit" is full of gravel or water, and the consequence of violently disturbing either of these can be readily imagined; and secondly, there is just the possibility of the bullet slipping slightly forward as the muzzle is pointed downwards; if it should start, a "bulge" would almost inevitably be the result. A wad placed *on the bullet* will avert this risk. He has never detected the advantage of firing off a bullet, and prefers simply squibbing into the pit, loading with the ordinary charge of powder and two wads only. It may be asked, Why then squib or do anything in the way of blowing off ? For this simple reason, that at the first discharge the barrel is not only absolutely clean, but contains no consumed products in the shape of fouling; consequently, in the first shot from a clean rifle the gases have the weight of the bullet *per se* to expel, whereas in subsequent shots there is the additional weight of the fouling, swept into the breech by the wad which is placed upon the powder. The weight of these products is more considerable than generally believed. In every charge of powder there are $^4/_{10}$ for gases and $^6/_{10}$ for solid products. The greater portion of the latter is blown out at each discharge, but enough remains to be worthy of consideration.

Having "blown-off," commence to load in earnest. Put on the false muzzle, half cock the rifle, pour in the powder, place one wad *quite square* in the false muzzle, and gently push it home with a steady uninterrupted sweep; give it two or three moderate taps, then push the bullet home in like manner, and give it also one or two slight taps; withdraw the rod and remove the false muzzle. The loading rod should, after three or four shots have been fired, be marked for both powder and bullet for guidance in loading. Do not cap till in position.

Firing.— As you are about to lie down in position, take a good look round and observe how the elements are comporting themselves. Do not judge by the appearance of one flag only; draw your inferences from the study of several. Having estimated the force of the wind, arrange your wind-gauge and proceed to fire as soon as possible. Keep your senses on the *qui vive.* Should any sudden change in the wind occur while aiming, do not hesitate to lower your rifle and make certain that your allowance is correct; if not, alter accordingly, but avoid the common fault of being too slow.

MATCH RIFLE SHOOTING.

Much harm results from losing the golden opportunity by unnecessarily faddling with one's sights. Before pulling the trigger, concentrate the whole attention on the shot, and let off, if possible, in the middle of the bull's-eye. Sometimes, for slight changes of wind on a shifting, variable day, it is better to borrow on the target; a foot or so can readily be allowed for with any sight except the solid aperture.

Having fired, don't lie expectantly on the firing-point, but get up and permit the next man to take his place. Much valuable time is wasted by the senseless habit some have of kicking their heels together till the shot has been signalled. If telescopes be allowed, it is well to notice accurately where the shot has struck. Proceed to load again as soon as possible, as the rifle loads better than after a delay of some minutes. Never get flurried; excitement is likely to lead to many errors. Method and placidity should be cultivated. Avoid talking, and do not worry about the doings and scores of others. Attend to the loading, and watch the wind; these two operations suffice fully to occupy all the time between the shots.

Light.— There is much superstition upon this point. Many pamphlets on Snider rifle shooting treat of the subject with a solemnity quite unnecessary. Curious arguments and facts (so-called) appear in juxtaposition, the result generally being the complete mystification of the reader, probably due to the similar condition of the author ! All the real effects produced by variations are due to the clearness or obscurity of the targets, and not, as some have scientifically stated, to the visual change of *position* of the targets. Anyhow, the small-bore man need not worry himself about this vexed point. If he attends to the wind question, he will soon find out what it is that causes variations in the angle of aim.

Diagrams.— Here personal taste must dictate. Some men elaborate volumes, while others hardly keep a record of any kind. The beginner, perhaps, should note rather carefully the results of his shots in order to cultivate a spirit of observation, but once this is attained, the notes had better be brief. The interval between each shot would be better spent in noting the various changes in the wind than in elaborate diagrams, etc. When trying experiments, of course it is most necessary to record every detail, but not so in competitive shooting.

THE THREE RIFLES.

Mishaps.— These will happen, and it may therefore be well to remark upon some of those most likely to occur. Firing without a bullet is by no means a rare occurrence. With the Metford rifle this act of omission appears in no way to affect the next shot, therefore it is unnecessary to do more than proceed to load as usual. The rifle will make a bull's-eye next shot if properly held. Two charges of powder may accidentally be fired with one bullet. When this happens, the bullet of course travels a long way over the target, and the barrel fouls considerably. It is necessary, therefore, to load, using three or four wads, after which pass an oiled rag down once or twice, and squib into the pit. Now load as usual, and the rifle will be found to act satisfactorily. All such misadventures generally arise from talking while loading; many a first prize has been lost in consequence. *Care* and some labour are never thrown away in rifle shooting — what is worth doing at all is worth doing *well*.

Positions.— There are so many, both prone (face) and back, that it would be wearisome to describe each in detail; it will, therefore, suffice to enumerate only those which are best calculated to produce good results. The reader, however, must bear in mind that, in the selection of a position, the primary consideration should have reference to personal construction ! A stout and corpulent rifleman can hardly hope to attempt, with success, the double-jointed contortions of his lean brother; he must, therefore, content himself with the choice of the best position of those within his capability. Very probably the face position, in some form, would, to him, prove most comfortable, and comfort is everything. The slim man, on the other hand, being capable of twisting his body into any attitude, may well hesitate before he too hastily denounces a position on account of its physical difficulties. Perseverance and practice are likely to insure success; a determined trial should therefore be given to any position which would seem likely to yield good results.

The prone, or face position, has less variations than the back position, the differences consisting chiefly in the angle the body is placed at in reference to the targets. From the perpendicular to an angle of 60° would include nearly the whole. The question of angle is of little moment. Every one should judge for himself which insures most ease and comfort. The elbows should be kept tolerably close to each other, the left elbow (when shooting from the right shoulder) being about ten inches in advance of the right, and three or four inches to its left. The left hand should grasp the rifle firmly as far forward as possible without unduly straining any of the muscles of the forearm. The right hand should gripe the small of the butt, and the forefinger be hooked round the trigger.

It is always desirable to have a solid basis of support — something rough enough to prevent the elbows slipping when the recoil of the rifle takes place. If cocoa-nut fibre mats be allowed they afford an excellent pad, but when mother earth alone is available it is well to avoid all inequalities, and if the ground be hard and slippery, the spots where the elbows will rest may be made somewhat more tolerable by one or two vigorous blows from the heel of one's boot.   Whatever the nature of the firing point, the chief consideration should be to get the elbows *firmly* planted before firing.

The general practice is to cross the legs over each other.   Some few keep them wide apart, while a smaller number still draw the right leg up as far as they conveniently can, in order to relieve the right lung of some of the pressure of the body's weight.   The following sketches illustrate three of the face positions :—

The "back position" had not found much favour until very lately, owing to the eccentric results it sometimes yields. Its *steadiness* cannot be questioned, but despite the apparent immovability of the barrel, while aiming, very often a wild shot is registered. These curious phenomena are doubtless due to *change of position* between shots. It is a well-known fact that the rifle behaves differently under different conditions. Supposing the barrel to be rested on a sandbag, with the point of contact, say, half-way up the barrel, and a series of shots fired, this diagram would materially differ from another, during the shooting of which the point of contact had been altered, say, one foot. The muscles of the neck are so unaccustomed to the peculiar strain, that it requires a long training to feel really comfortable while firing, but with patient practice all these difficulties may be overcome. The Americans, who adopt two or three distinctly different back positions, made some marvellous scores in their matches against the Irish, Scotch, and imperial teams. One disadvantage, and it is a somewhat serious one, is the impossibility of scrutinizing the flags, whilst aiming, as readily as when on the face.

Assuming, then, the back position to be a good one, which, from among the many, should be adopted ? Here, again, the man's physical build must, in a great measure, decide the selection. But as almost all the back positions are somewhat difficult at first, no one should hastily abandon them; a fair trial is necessary. Sergeant-Instructor Gilder is perhaps one of our most successful back-shots. Captain Pearce, the Gold Medallist, won his laurels in this position. Many of the "Eights," too, shoot on their backs, and make excellent shooting. It must be conceded, therefore, that in its many modifications it can be made to yield good results. Without honouring any of the varieties by calling them by the names of those who successfully adopt them, it will answer all practical purposes to describe a few which seem to be amongst the best.

I.

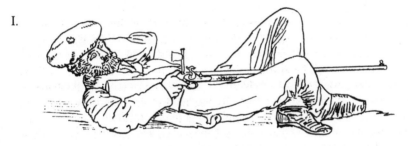

I.   Lie on the broad of the back; draw up both knees, pinching the left shank-bone with the right calf, so as to form a V-shaped bed, wherein to rest the barrel; pass the left arm round the back of the head, and firmly hold the nape of the neck in order to support the head; lay the barrel of the rifle in the V formed by the legs; grasp "the small" with the right hand, and draw the "heel-plate" into the right armpit, at the same time slightly turning on to the right side. Now glance through the sights, and ascertain whether the legs are crossed so as to support the rifle in the proper line for the aim. If the muzzle be too high, lower it by allowing the legs to open out a little; if it be too low, raise the muzzle by closing the legs somewhat more.

Full cock and take the final aim, being careful to watch the bubble to see if the sights be *upright*. The breathing must be suspended just before pressing the trigger, and until the rifle has exploded.

II.

II.   Lie on the back; draw up the left leg sufficiently so as to be nearly upright from the knee to the ankle; cross or hook the right leg round the shank-bone of the left leg, pinching it with the bend (inside) of the right knee; pass the left hand round the head until the tips of the fingers touch the ground; rest the head firmly on the forearm and wrist; lay the barrel of the rifle on the projection formed by the bend of the right knee, keeping it clear of the left leg; grasp the "small of the butt," and draw the "heel-plate" into the right armpit. Glance through the sights, and ascertain if the rifle be properly elevated; if it be raised too high, lower the right knee; if it be too low, lift the right knee, but be careful not to relinquish a tight hold of the left shank-bone. Now brace up for the final aim, and, with restrained breath, steadily press the trigger until the rifle explodes.

III.   Lie on the back; draw up the left leg as far as possible with comfort; cross or hook the right leg round the left shank-bone, pinching it with the inside bend of the right knee; lay the barrel of the rifle on the projection formed by the bend of the right knee, holding the "small" firmly with the right hand; pass the left arm round the head, and seize the "heel-plate" of the rifle, the left thumb being near the right ear, and the remaining fingers round the opposite side of the rifle-stock. The toe of the heel-plate

III.

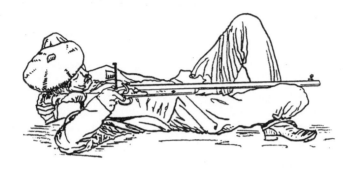

should project an inch or more beyond the right shoulder, and the right arm should rest firmly on the ground, being at the same time nearly at a right angle to the body; the back of the neck should rest on the back part of the "comb" (some men prefer resting the cheek). Glance through the sights, and either raise or lower the right knee until the aim be correct. The left hand should retain a *firm* hold of the heel-plate to control the recoil. After some practice *heavy* charges may be fired with impunity; but the beginner should proceed with caution, using but small charges at first. Indeed, it is preferable to commence by using powder *only* for a few shots, until the nature of the recoil be properly understood, when a bullet may be fired. The trigger guard is apt, at first, to damage the middle finger; a strip of chamois leather, ¾ of an inch wide and about 9 inches long, wound round and round the finger and then stitched at the sides, forms an excellent pad, and can be drawn on and off the finger at pleasure. It is superior to the rubber pads sold by gun-makers, as *oil* does not spoil it.

IV.

IV.   Lie full length on the ground, turning somewhat on to the right side; keep the right leg straight, and cross the left leg over it, the feet being close to each other.   Lay the barrel of the rifle on the thigh, just above the knee, draw the heel of the stock into the right armpit, pass the left arm round the head, and rest the tips of the fingers upon the ground, so as to form a support for the head.   Align the rifle on the target, and gently squeeze the trigger , as in the other positions.   Those who adopt this position state that, to avoid being punished by the recoil, it is desirable not to press the butt too tightly into the armpit — only just draw it in without using force.   If the line of aim should need being altered, it must be principally done by raising or depressing the heel of the rifle-stock. A slight change, too, in the position of the barrel, either higher up or lower down on the left leg, may be necessary.

In all the back positions, if *short* rifles be used, great care should always be observed to have the *muzzle* projecting *beyond* the knee; should the tip of the muzzle be actually resting on the knee at the moment of explosion, the consequences would be *very serious*.

The orthoptic, in positions 1, 2, and 4, is too far from the eye to allow of the use of the ordinary ($\cdot$05) size aperture.   The correct size must depend upon circumstances.   The rule that should regulate the selection is, to be able *to see clearly* while aiming.   Some, from peculiarity of sight, can see better through a small aperture, while others cannot do without a larger one. But for those who have had no experience in the matter, and who must order from their gunmakers prior to practice, it may be useful to state that, as a general rule, the best size for the aperture, in the face position, is $\cdot$05; for the back position, $\cdot$09, or even $\cdot$10.

Some riflemen have the orthoptic removed from the small, and placed on the heel of the rifle, so as to have the aperture close to the eye; but this has its disadvantages.   The strain on the stock at each shot is very considerable, and it is too much to demand, even of the best seasoned piece of wood, that it should remain absolutely rigid.   The fact is, the stock is collared, more or less, by the recoil, and gets deflected.   Consequently, the orthoptic at the extreme end of the butt is affected, and the aim is gradually altered, the result of which would be painfully manifest in case a long interval should occur between two shots, as sometimes happens when a shot is disputed, and the firing stopped for a time. The writer, therefore, prefers leaving the orthoptic in its usual place, and meeting the change of position by introducing a considerably larger aperture.

Trajectory.— It is of importance to know something of the curves described by bullets during their flight from the rifle to the target. A rifleman thoroughly acquainted with the performance of his weapon, and having confidence in himself, could apply his knowledge with absolute certainty in actual warfare, when it might be desirable to open fire at the enemy *over the heads of intermediate troops.* The "culminating point"— that is, the highest point above the line of vision or aim— attained by the bullet may, for all practical purposes, up to 1000 yards, be stated to be half-way; *i.e.* when firing at 600 yards, the "culminating point" would be at or about 300 yards; at 1000 yards, at or about 500 yards, and so on. The process by which to ascertain the exact height of the bullet at its "culminating point" is not over difficult, and may be stated thus :—

(1.) Take the angle of elevation for the required distance, convert this angle into feet for that distance, and divide the value by two.

(2.) Then take from the tables the angle of elevation for half of the given distance, and convert this angle into feet for half of the given distance.

(3.) Lastly, subtract the latter amount from the former, and the result will be the height of the trajectory, sufficiently near for all practical purposes; *e.g.* suppose it were necessary to ascertain the height of the "culminating point" with the Metford Match rifle, with 1000 yards elevation, the above rule would be thus applied :—

(1.) Referring to the tables, we find the angle of elevation for 1000 yards (required distance) to be 2° 20' ; this, reduced to minutes, would be 140'. For convenience in calculating, it is assumed that a minute equals one inch for every hundred yards, and therefore, at 1000 yards, a minute would represent 10 inches (though really it equals 10·47 inches); 140' then multiplied by 10 (inches) equals 1400 inches, or 116 feet 8 inches. This value, divided by 2, gives 58 feet 4 inches.

(2.) From the same tables, we find the angle of elevation for 500 yards (half of the given distance, 1000 yards) to be 57½'. This, to be converted into feet, must be brought into inches first, by being multiplied by 5 (*i.e.*

one for each of the 100 yards in 500 yards), which equals 288 inches (nearly), or 24 feet.

(3.) The latter amount, 24 feet, must now be subtracted from the former 58 feet 4 inches, which leaves 34 feet 4 inches for the height of the culminating point.

Briefly recapitulated in *figures*, the calculation stands thus :—

$$2° 20' \text{ (angle for 1000 yards.)}$$

$$\underline{60}$$

$$140' \text{ (minutes.)}$$

$$\underline{\quad 10}$$

$$12\underline{)\,1400} \text{ inches.}$$

$$2\underline{)\,116 \text{ ft. 8 in.}}$$

$$58 \text{ ft. } 4 \text{ in.}$$

$$57\tfrac{1}{2}' \text{ (angle for 500 yards.)}$$

$$\underline{\quad 5}$$

$$12\underline{)\;287·5} \text{ inches.}$$

$$23 \text{ ft. } 11\tfrac{1}{2} \text{ in.} \text{ — say 24 feet.}$$

	ft.	in.
	58	4
	24	0
	34	4	(height of culminating point.)

Another method is as follows :—

Subtract the angle of the shorter range (half of the required distance) from the angle of the given distance, and convert the remainder into feet — *e.g.* :

$$2° 20' \quad \text{(angle for 1000 yards, given distance.)}$$

$$\underline{\quad 57\tfrac{1}{2}'} \text{ (angle for 500 yards, half of given distance, 1000 yards.)}$$

$$1° 22\tfrac{1}{2}' \text{ — remainder.}$$

$$\underline{60}$$

$$82\tfrac{1}{2}' \text{ (minutes.)}$$

$$\underline{\quad 5}$$

$$12\underline{)\,412·5} \text{ inches.}$$

$$34 \text{ ft. } 4\tfrac{1}{2} \text{ in. (Height of culminating point.)}$$

As already stated, the culminating point may, for practical purposes, be taken as being *very nearly mid-way*. In angles so flat as are used in rifle shooting, the tangents are so very nearly their radii that they may be regarded as equal. The following taken up to 4°, or, say, 1500 yards, will illustrate the truth of the assertion :—

	Arc.	Sine.	Tangent.
1°	·0174533	·0174524	·0174551
2°	·0349066	·0348995	·0349208
3°	·0523599	·0523360	·0524078
4°	·0698132	·0697565	·0699268

The popular notion regarding the course described by rifle bullets is that they travel over a course somewhat like the accompanying outline, at the longer distances :—

Rifle's muzzle, A ; target, B.

This is very fallacious. The curve is always a curve, quickening more and more, it is true, but nothing like the above, not even when the spherical ball was used. Another popular idea is that the course described by the rifle bullet at, say, 1000 yards, is considerably more than the actual distance the target may be from the rifleman. What the difference may be is not opined, but that it is considerable is confidently asserted. The true answer may not therefore be out of place while considering this question of curves. At 1000 yards the flight of the bullet will measure scarcely *one foot more, i.e.* 1000¹/₃ yards; the difference being very insignificant.

The annexed tables will show the height of the "culminating point" for every hundred yards from 200 to 1000. The heights given for the Snider are taken from the "Field Exercises" and "Musketry Instruction;" the writer cannot, therefore, vouch for their accuracy.

THE THREE RIFLES.

Metford Match Rifle

Distance Yards	Particulars of Work.			Ft.	in..		Ft.	in.	Height Culminating Point	Ft.	in.
200 ...	20' × 2 ÷ 2 ÷ 12 =			1	8	—	0	10	=	0	10
300 ...	31½' × 3 ÷ 2 ÷ 12 =			3	11	—	1	10	=	2	1
400 ...	44' × 4 ÷ 2 ÷ 12 =			7	4	—	3	4	=	4	0
500 ...	57½' × 5 ÷ 2 ÷ 12 =			12	0	—	5	4	=	6	8
600 ...	72' × 6 ÷ 2 ÷ 12 =			18	0	—	7	10	=	10	2
700 ...	87½' × 7 ÷ 2 ÷ 12 =			25	6	—	10	11	=	14	7
800 ...	104' × 8 ÷ 2 ÷ 12 =			34	8	—	14	8	=	20	0
900 ...	120½' × 9 ÷ 2 ÷ 12 =			45	7	—	19	0	=	26	7
1000 ...	140' × 10 ÷ 2 ÷ 12 =			58	4	—	24	0	=	34	4

Old Enfield Rifle.

200		1	3
300		3	0
400		5	8
500		10	0
600		15	0
700		21	8
800		30	8
900		41	8
1000		55	6

Snider (vide "Musketry Instruction" and "Field Exercises")

200		5	0
300		7	0
400		11	0
500		15	0
600		23	0
700		32	0
800		44	0

Zero.— As no two men hardly will shoot the same rifle alike, it is almost impossible for any gunmaker to send out all his rifles zeroed to suit every one. Hence it happens that one man finds his zero for elevation too favourable, another that his is just the other way. It is rather a nuisance to feel uncertain on this point, and it is therefore a good plan, on a *calm* day, to shoot the rifle at 100 yards, and note how far it differs, if at all, from the "scale" of elevations. This will settle the question, and by either adding or subtracting the difference from the several printed angles, the "scale" may be made absolutely correct.

The ingenious inventor of the rifle, in order to meet this requirement, has devised a *shifting* zero, whereby an alteration of a few minutes may be made, and the angles be still kept at the values given in the printed tables. But the manufacturer does not seem to have introduced it very freely, and those desirous of having it must especially order that the orthoptic be fitted with a "shifting zero."

If the rifle be "dead set" at 200 yards, it will have a drift of 30 inches to the right at 1000 yards. This drift, however, may be overcome by causing the back-sight to incline two-hundredths of an inch to the left at 2°, or 900 yards elevation, by which means the rifle will shoot nearly straight (*i.e.* with hardly any drift) at all the distances in use amongst riflemen.

Should this arrangement be impracticable, it will always be necessary to make the required allowance for the natural drift of the bullet, deducting the value from the supposed necessary allowance for a right wind (*i.e.* blowing from right to left,) and adding it when the wind blows from the left; *e.g.* if a rifle arranged so as to shoot "*straight*" at 1000 yards requires, say, 10 feet of allowance for a wind from the right, then the rifle with the 30 inches drift will only require 7 feet 6 inches allowance on its wind-gauge, because 7 feet 6 inches plus 2 feet 6 inches (drift) equals 10 feet altogether.

Some riflemen are so situated that it may not be convenient to take a rifle to the range and test its zero at 100 yards, as suggested.

Another way of ascertaining it will therefore be described.

Procure a piece of cardboard, say, 12 inches × 8 inches (any moderate size will do,) and rule a couple of lines three inches apart through its greatest width.

On these lines draw circular bull's-eyes the size of the *base* of the bullet; four bull's-eyes on each line, so as to leave a fair margin on both sides; thus :—

12 in.

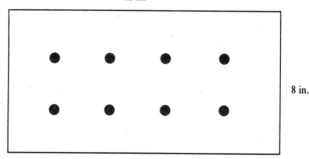

8 in.

Place this cardboard target against a mound of earth, fagots of wood, or anything sufficiently dense to stop the bullets. It is safer to shoot with a wall behind to prevent the possibility of an accident. If the wall alone be available, loose earth or some bundles of straw should be placed between it and the cardboard target, as the match rifle punishes a wall pretty considerably; moreover, the lead splinters might injure the shooter if no such precautions were adopted. Having arranged the above target a few inches above the ground, measure off 12 yards from the target to where the *muzzle* will be when firing. Load as usual, and screw the back-sight down to the *nominal* zero, and set the foresight "*dead on.*" Aim at the left-hand bull's-eye on the upper line. If the zero be correct, the bullet should strike ten-eighths($^{10}/_8$) of an inch, *i.e.* 1¼ inches, *below* the bull's-eye, and about two-eighths ($^2/_8$), or ¼ of an inch, to the *left*. Fire five or six shots before finally deciding, for though the distance be exceedingly short, it is by no means difficult to make bad shooting ! It therefore requires a few shots to determine the accurate zero. After five or six shots have been fired, measure with a foot rule from the centre of the bull's-eyes to the centre of the bullet-holes (the upper or lower edge of the bull's-eye will answer equally well, provided the same part of the bullet-hole be taken,) and note if the average readings will give the required result, *viz.* $^{10}/_8$ of an inch *below* the bull's-eye, and $^2/_8$ of an inch to the *left*. If such be the case, the zero is correct; but if the measurements differ, the zero must be corrected, either by raising or lowering the sight, until the proper position of the shots be obtained, and this difference, either added to or subtracted from the printed tables, will be the true reading for the rifle in the hands of that particular rifleman.

Every minute equals $\frac{1}{8}$ of an inch at 12 yards. Should the measurement be, say, $\frac{12}{8}$ instead of $\frac{10}{8}$ of an inch, it is evident that the zero must be two minutes understated, and it would be necessary to *add* two minutes throughout to the printed angles, in order to make true shooting. But if, on the other hand, the measurements were found to be, say, $\frac{7}{8}$ of an inch, it would be equally evident that the zero must be *overstated* three minutes, and it would be necessary to deduct three minutes from the several angles throughout the "scale." The lateral zero must be treated in like manner.

The inquiring mind will naturally desire to know the principles upon which these rules are based, which are as follows :— At 12 yards the fall by gravity is one-eighth ($\frac{1}{8}$) of an inch, and it so happens that $\frac{1}{8}$ of an inch equals one minute (1'), or one-hundredth of an inch nearly at 12 yards; for one inch equals one minute at 95·49 yards, and 95·49 yards divided by 8 gives 11·93 yards, which is so close upon 12 yards, that it may practically be considered as representing 12 yards.

Every foot rule is divided into eighths of an inch, and each of these divisions of $\frac{1}{8}$ may therefore be regarded as *minutes*, for by that means the true zero may be ascertained without the labour of elaborate calculations. The simple measuring with a foot rule is all that is necessary to apply the formula.

The bore of the rifle is $\frac{9}{8}$ of an inch below the "sight line;" the drop due to gravity, $\frac{1}{8}$ of an inch. These two added together ($\frac{9}{8} + \frac{1}{8}$) equal $\frac{10}{8}$, or the measurement to the spot *below* where the bullet should strike, if the zero be correct.

THE THREE RIFLES.

Batch of Receipts.— To "dead black" sights. Any sights, which are not fixed to the rifle, may, when worn bright, be made a dead black thus :— Take of

Nitric acid	...	...	...	1 part
Water ...	...	...	...	7 parts

Thoroughly mix, and the solution will be ready for use.

Detach from the rifle the part that needs to be operated upon, and with a fine piece of emery cloth thoroughly brighten the surface. Place the piece of metal in boiling water (a teacupful,) to which a pinch of bicarbonate of soda has been added, and stir it about briskly with a strip of iron wire, glass rod, or stick. After a few minutes pour off the water, and add more boiling water without soda; treat as before, and drain off the water. The object of this process is to remove all traces of grease, which is an enemy to perfect success.

Take of the nitric acid solution as much as will thoroughly cover the sight or sights that have to be blackened — an old wine-glass, damaged coffee-cup, or any such vessel answers admirably for holding the acid mixture. Drop the sights in one by one, being careful that no two get into close contact, as it is necessary that the acid should have free access to the surfaces. After a few seconds the bright polished surface will assume a dull leaden look, and the fluid will become slightly discoloured immediately around the metal. Gradually the smooth look will give place to a *finely pitted* appearance, when the sight should be turned over. In about three minutes the action of the acid should have been sufficiently marked, when the sights must be removed, being dragged out with a hairpin or wire; at once plunge them into a small vessel filled with *boiling* water(an empty salt jar is as good as any vessel). Stir them about briskly, pour off the water, and fill again with *boiling* water; allow them to remain in about five minutes; now remove them, and put them to *boil* in an old saucepan for 15 or 20 minutes, in order to kill every trace of acid. If the washing be hurried over, the chances are that red spots and streaks will appear in the next step.

After wiping the sights with a dry cloth, proceed to blacken as follows :—

Twist a piece of iron wire round the sight, to manipulate with; hold it in a gas flame, and carefully watch the *colour*.   At first it will turn straw colour, then brown, after that dark brown, and lastly a bluish colour, when it should be removed and plunged into oil (salad oil, so called, answers well). If allowed to pass the bluish colour, it will become white with heat, and this is undesirable.   After allowing it to cool in the oil, remove it, and the black ought to be "dead" — i.e. not shining — due to the finely pitted surface breaking up the light that might otherwise be reflected.

Another way is to heat the metal till it is *nearly* red-hot, and then plunge it into oil.   When cool, wipe it thoroughly and heat again and dip into oil, and so on until the proper depth of colour be obtained.   But this method is not so *clean* in its result as the first-named, which, if carefully done, should be quite black enough.   Where the gas flame is not available, a red-hot poker will answer — the sight to be *laid* on the red-hot poker and watched during the colouring process.   Even a candle will do as a make-shift.

Temporary Dead Black.— A capital black may be made at a trifling cost; it is far superior to what is sold.   It is made thus :—

1 oz. "Stick-lac" ...	...	...	cost about 3d.	
1 ” vegetable black	...	...	”	0¼
6 ” methylated spirit	...	...		6
				———
				9¼d.

Dissolve the "stick-lac" in the methylated spirit (it takes about a week to melt thoroughly), then strain it through muslin and add the vegetable black, shaking up the contents of the bottle to insure a thorough mixing.   It may happen that, owing to slight differences in the materials, a little more or less than the stated quantity of the vegetable black may be necessary.   This must be judged by the consistency of the mixture when applied.   Cork it down tight, and fill a small bottle from time to time, as required for immediate use.

The above quantity, costing 9¼d., is equal to about six shillings' worth of "sight-black," as sold at Wimbledon and elsewhere, and is vastly superior, for this excellent reason — that it is almost *difficult* to rub it off, whereas we all know to our cost how easily the ordinary "sight-black" may be brushed off. The "stick-lac" is the binding ingredient, and should be increased in quantity if the black, after being made, should not seem sufficiently tenacious.

Castings of the Breech.— For scientific purposes, it may occasionally be necessary to have a perfect knowledge of the formation of the chambering of the breech, and this can only be obtained by *castings*. There are several ways of getting these —

1. By using molten lead.
2.   "   melted wax.
3.   "   plaster of Paris.
4.   "   melted sulphur.

The last-named is unquestionably the simplest and best, and yields a most beautiful casting.

Take of common stick sulphur sufficient for the required purpose, place it in an iron lead-ladle, melt it on the fire, and when liquid, pour it into the chamber. It cools almost immediately, and can be readily taken out. A cleaning rod, with some tow on the jag, should be pushed down from muzzle to breech, and checked when within an inch of the chamber; invert the rifle (muzzle downwards) and pour in the melted sulphur. The casting, when removed, will show the chamber, the entry into the barrel, and about an inch of the rifling, and will present a perfectly smooth surface, with an exact impression of the inside. To get out the casting, it is only necessary to return the rifle to its ordinary position and push the rod home, which will expel the sulphur casting.

Kicking.— Many a competitor's cheek bears painful marks of the punishment inflicted by the kick of the rifle at 200 yards. The remedy is both simple and efficacious. With a rough file remove about $\frac{1}{16}$ of an inch from off the "comb" of the rifle, more particularly where the cheekbone rests, and slope it, in a workmanlike manner, towards the "small." Lastly, with a piece of sand-paper, smooth the surface until all traces of the file have disappeared; a little linseed oil well rubbed in, will restore the wood to its original colour. The alteration is so slight that the eye cannot detect it afterwards, if well done. The comfort, in being spared continued bruises, amply repays for the slight trouble entailed.

Pull-off of Trigger.— It may happen that a heavy or light "pull-off" requires to be altered, and no one competent to undertake the work within reach. In such instances, it might prove of great value to know how to remedy the evil. It may be done thus :—

Remove the lock — full cock — place the clamp (a particular instrument for this especial purpose) on the main-spring, and screw it up tight; uncock by pressing the projecting arm of the sear; partly unscrew the "sear-spring pin" (one complete turn suffices), and insert the edge of the screw-driver between the bend of the sear-spring and the lock-plate, until the stud of the former be released. Unscrew the sear-pin, and remove the sear. Unscrew the bridle-pin, and remove the bridle. Remove the hammer. Remove the tumbler — the piece to be operated upon.

With a fine file, lightly pass a few strokes across the "full-bent" *A* (sketch *WW*), sloping the edge towards the half bent *B*, as in sketch *Y* (drawn on a *very* magnified scale, to indicate clearly the direction in which the filing must be done). *Ever so little* filing materially alters the pull-off, caution must therefore be observed.

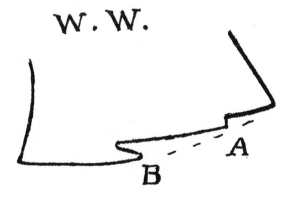

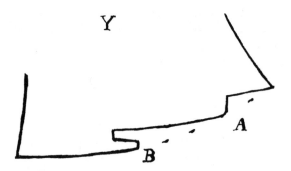

The eye should scarcely be able to detect the alteration.   After filing, take a flat piece of "Turkey stone" and oil, and polish the surface by gentle friction, to prevent any drag.   Put the lock together, and test the pull-off, which may be done with ordinary weights and a piece of cord attached to a light wooden rod.

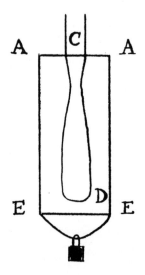

MATCH RIFLE SHOOTING.

The bar *A A* to be placed across the trigger at *C*, and the weights to hang a few inches below the heel-plate *D*, the cord to be kept from contact with the stock by means of notched bar at *E E*.   By adding or removing pounds, or half-pounds the exact pull-off may be ascertained.

Some gunmakers file the nose of the sear; this entails much less trouble, and may be adopted for this reason.

Foresight.— The military foresight may occasionally, from wear or other causes, become *bright*.   It can easily be darkened by applying three or four common *sulphur matches* in quick succession.   The fumes of the sulphur, in conjunction with the heat of the flame, act upon the metal, and by rubbing on a little oil the process is completed.   A very fair black should result.

Bichloride of Platina will also make a very fair black.   The foresight, or whatever part needs the operation, must first be polished with flour-emery cloth, after which apply the bichloride of platina with a stick (a wooden match answers).   Continue the application until the metal be sufficiently black, after which wash with water, and dry; finally oil.   The success of this method would seem to depend upon the bichloride of platina.   It must be strong and pure.

CHAPTER V.

MATCH - RIFLE SHOOTING — BREECH - LOADER.

THE coming Wimbledon of 1878 will be the first occasion on which Match breech-loaders will figure in any numbers, and to judge by their performances so far, there is every reason to believe the standard of their shooting will be equal to any on record.   Those most likely to attract attention are the Metford, the Remington, and the Sharp.   The merits of the English and Yankee weapons have been somewhat hotly discussed in the pages of the *Volunteer Service Gazette,* but it is doubtful whether the outside public have been able to form any conclusions.   Therefore, the actual performance of the English and American rifles will be a matter of interest to all riflemen, and as some of the best shots of the day will do battle with these respective weapons in the public contests of Wimbledon, it is to be hoped that the merits of each class of rifle will be brought to light.

It is claimed that the American rifle is, *par excellence,* the best of the day, but the evidence of this assertion is of too slender a character to be of value.   When it is borne in mind that the present system of rifling originated in this country, *viz.* the *hardened* cylindrical projectile and shallow creasing, the superiority of the American weapons can only be based upon the assumption of superiority of mere mechanical workmanship; and, though admitting the excellence of all Yankee mechanism, it is too much to suppose that our rifle manufacturers are unable to compete against their transatlantic brethren.

The Americans unquestionably first publicly demonstrated that breech-loaders would shoot as well as muzzle-loaders.   While we Britishers struggled to get results of a high character out of a *fouled* breech-loader, and failed, the American, with that *sang froid* peculiar to him, coolly cleaned out his weapon between each discharge, scorning the smile that this operation naturally excited.

When, however, he proved his capacity to make bull's-eyes, the absurdity of the process lost its character;   and the result is that the "cleaning-out" system is now generally in vogue, the actual *modus operandi* differing slightly.

Whether such a system is worthy of adoption, is at present beside the question. The point at issue is : Which will shoot best — a breech-loader cleaned out, or a muzzle-loader ? Theoretically the former, but the practically has yet to be actually decided. The process of cleaning out must be carefully and scientifically conducted, else misadventures will result, but when this is really efficiently performed every time, the shooting is remarkably fine, and possibly, in a long race, the breech-loader would, in hot weather, beat the muzzle-loader. However, those who use the obsolete muzzle-loader need not just yet lay aside their tried and trusted pieces of steel.

Those who elect to use the breech-loader will find that the shooting will depend upon the *regularity* with which the wiping out after each shot is performed. It must always be alike. Some prefer slightly oiling the barrel after each cleaning out; others simply clean out carefully, omitting the oiling.

The process may thus be summed up : Have two rods — one with a brush and the other constructed to carry a piece of rag through a slot at one end, the other end cut like a jag to pass rags up and down. The brush is almost absolutely necessary in the American rifles which fire American powder, the fouling of which is very much more tenacious than that of English powder.

Having fired, remove the empty case. Moisten with the tongue a piece of swan's-down calico (1½ inch square), pass it *slowly* up the barrel from breech to muzzle until it just protrudes, then slowly draw it back, reverse it, and repeat the operation. Look through the barrel and observe if it be *quite clean* — no little hardened spots of fouling adhering to the barrel anywhere; if there be, they must be removed by repeating the operation. Sometimes one or two such specks will not yield to the swan's-down calico alone; the brush should then be passed through (dry) and drawn up and down two or three times, which will have the desired effect. When thoroughly clean, take a piece of swan's-down calico (1½ inch) slightly oiled, place it through the slot in the rod, then pass it slowly up and down, withdrawing with a *steady sweep*. Again look through and see that the barrel is in order, and *always the same*. When called upon to fire, get into position, and then insert the cartridge.

The rods should be marked so as to know when the muzzle has been reached. It is best to sit down and clean out with the rifle laid across the knees.

The cartridges are loaded exactly like those used in the Farquharson-Metford, excepting that the charge should be 90 grains No. 6 Curtis and Harvey's powder, one waxed wad, and 540 grains bullet. The Americans load their cartridges somewhat differently, and mostly prefer to use nothing between the powder and the bullet. Their charge is also nominally larger, but the powder is considerably weaker than Curtis and Harvey's.

All the rest of the manipulation is similar to that described under the Match muzzle-loader.

CHAPTER VI.

HISTORY OF SMALL - ARMS.

MUCH obscurity attaches itself to the EXACT date when fire-arms were first discovered. According to records contained in the chapter house, Westminster, mention is made of an attack on the manor house of Huntercombe, Yorkshire, in 1375, by forty men armed, among other weapons, with "gonnes" — supposed to be the hand-gun. We also read of the "arquebuse à Mèche" in Germany, in 1378, so that the invention probably occurred some years earlier. Gunpowder having been manufactured in England in 1346, it is not probable that the introduction of hand-guns could be of a later date, though it would seem they were not in general use till nearly a *century* after being invented !

The hand-gun was of very rude construction; it consisted of an iron or brass tube, with a touch-hole. This tube was fixed in a straight stock of wood, about a cubit † and a half long; it had no lock, and was fired by the application of a match. The shooting, as may be judged, was extremely inaccurate, even at close quarters.

During the reign of Henry VII an improvement in fire-arms took place. A cock was fixed to the hand-gun to hold the match, which was brought down to the priming by a trigger — whence the term matchlock; but so crude were all the contrivances for firing this equally crude hand-gun, that in 1580 one of the most remarkable men of the time, Michael Montaigne, in alluding to small-arms, writes thus :— "Except the noise in our ears, to which we will henceforth be accustomed, I think it is an arm of very little effect, and I hope that we shall one day give up its use." And somewhat later, other writers deplored the abandonment of the long-bow, and predicted the certain ruin of old England, whose bewitched sons only knew how to use fire-arms. Could the departed spirits of these worthies only return, and spend a fortnight on the Wimbledon Common during the rifle meeting, they would change the tone of their lamentations.

† [Mediæval measure based on the length of the fore-arm, usually 18 to 22 inches — Ed.]

THE THREE RIFLES.

The modern *flint-lock* was invented about 1635, but does not appear to have been used in England until 1677. The Earl of Orrery, in that year, describes the superiority of the flint-lock over the match-lock in the following words :— "First, it is exceedingly more ready; for with the fire-lock you have only to cock, and you are prepared to shoot; but with your match–lock you have several motions, the least of which is as long a-performing, as but that one of the other, and oftentimes much more hazardous; besides, if you fire not the match-lock musket as soon as you have blown your match (which often, especially in hedge fights and sieges, you cannot do), you must a second time blow your match, or the ashes it gathers hinders it from firing. Secondly, the match is very dangerous, either where the bandeleers are used, or where soldiers run hastily in fight to the budge-barrel, to refill their bandeleers; I have often seen sad instances thereof. Thirdly, marching in the nights, to avoid an enemy, or to surprise one, or to assault the fortress, the matches often discover you, and inform the enemy where you are, whereby you suffer much, and he obtains much. Fourthly, in wet weather, the pan of the musket being made wide open, for a while the rain often deadens the powder, and the match too; and in windy weather, blows away the powder, ere the match can touch the pan; nay, often in very high winds, I have often seen the sparks blown from the match, fire the musket ere the soldier meant it; and either thereby lose his shot, or wound or kill some one before him. Whereas in the fire-lock, the motion is so sudden, that what makes the cock fall on the hammer, strikes the fire, and opens the pan at once. Lastly, to omit many other reasons, the quantity of match used in an army does much add to the baggage, and being of a very dry quality, naturally draws the moisture of the air, which makes it relax, and consequently less fit, though carried in close waggons; but if you march without waggons, the match is the more exposed; and without being dried again in ovens, is but of half the use which otherwise it would be of; and which is full as bad, the skeans you give the corporals, and the links you give the private soldiers (of which near an enemy, or on ordinary guard duty, they must never be unfurnished), if they lodge in huts or tents, or if they keep guard in the open field (as most often it happens), all the match for instant service is too often rendered uncertain or useless. Nothing of all which can be said of the flint, but much of it to the contrary. And then the soldiers generally wearing their links of match near the bottom of the belt, on which their bandeleers are fastened, in wet weather generally spoil the match they have, and if they are to fight on a sudden, and in the rain, you lose the use of your small shot, which is sometimes of irreparable prejudice."

The objections to the flint-lock were that it did not entirely preserve the priming from the wet, and that the flint sometimes failed to ignite the charge. In 1807 Alexander John Forsyth obtained a patent for priming with fulminating powder, which, when struck with any metal or hard substance, exploded. At first this compound was made of chlorate of potash, sulphur, and charcoal, but being too corrosive was subsequently improved upon. In 1834 Mr. Forsyth's invention was tested at Woolwich against flint-lock muskets; the trial resulted in favour of the percussion principle, consequently the flint-lock muskets were all converted to be fired by the percussion cap, containing the detonating composition, now made of three parts of chlorate of potash, two of fulminate of mercury, and one of powdered glass.

In 1842 a model musket, on the percussion principle, was adopted, with a block or back-sight for 150 yards; the size of the bore being ·753, and the charge of powder 4½ drachms.

The shooting powers of this weapon are shown by the results of the experimental firing at Chatham in 1846, the report upon which concludes thus:—

"It appears by these experiments that, as a general rule, musketry fire should never be opened beyond 150 yards, and certainly not exceeding 200 yards; at this distance half the number of shots missed the target 11 ft. 6 in., and at 150 yards a very large proportion also missed; at 75 and 100 yards every shot struck the target 2 feet wide, and had the deviation increased simply as the distance, every shot ought to have struck the target 6 feet wide at 200 yards; instead of this, however, some were observed to pass several yards to the right or left, some to fall 30 yards short, and others to pass as much beyond, and the deviation increased in a still greater degree as the range increased.   It is only, then, under peculiar circumstances, such as when it may be desirable to bring a fire on field artillery, when there are no other means of replying to it, that it ought ever to be thought of using the musket at such distances as 400 yards."

Such was the value of the weapon used by the British soldier, until its use was partially superseded, in 1851, by the Minié rifle, and altogether by the Enfield rifle in 1855.

The invention of rifling has been attributed to Gaspard Zoller, or Zollner, of Vienna, about the end of the 15th century.   It is supposed that the grooves, which at first were *straight*, were cut in order to receive and so decrease the effect of the fouling.   They also tended to increase the accuracy of the shooting, as the bullet was at least directed in a straight line down the barrel.

About the year 1520, Koster of Nuremberg is stated to have adopted the spiral form of grooving.   Whether he understood the value of this change, or merely accidentally stumbled upon it, seems uncertain.

In the official catalogue of the Tower Armouries, it is stated that "rifling barrels commenced about the beginning of the 17th century, and the earliest patent in the Patent Office for rifling small-arms was granted to Arnold Rotsipen, and is dated 24th June, 1635, and reads as follows :— To draw or to shave barrells for pieces of all sortes, straight, even, and smooth, and to make anie crooked barrell perfectly straight with greate ease, and to *rifle*, cutt out, or screwe barrells as wyde, or as close, or as deepe, or as shallowe as shall be required, with greate ease."

In the Tower may be seen some specimens of rifles bearing dates 1610 - 1613 and 1630.

In 1800 the 95th Regiment, now Rifle Brigade was armed with the "Baker rifle."   The barrel was 30 inches long, and had seven grooves, with a pitch of one turn in ten feet, or a quarter turn in the length of the barrel; the calibre was 20.   As spherical bullets were used, it was necessary to have the bullet somewhat larger than the bore;   hence the loading was always a difficult and tedious operation, more especially after the rifle had been fouled by firing;   for which reason rifled weapons were not considered as

74

convenient as the smooth-bore.   Several efforts were made by different inventors to introduce some plan to overcome the difficulties of loading, but with no marked success.

In William IV.'s reign the Brunswick rifle was introduced into the army. The barrel was 30 inches long, and had two grooves, with a pitch of one turn in 2 ft. 6 in.   The bullet was spherical, with a belt to fit the grooves, and weighed 557 grains.   The shooting was never good, and beyond 400 yards very uncertain.

The adoption of a serviceable rifled arm remained a vexed question until 1847, when Captain Minié suggested that an iron cup should be introduced into the base of the bullet, which was considered a practical and definite solution of the principle of expansion.

The form of the bullet first used with the English Minié rifle was conoidal, but as there was little chance of the axis of the bullet coinciding with that of the barrel during its passage out, the defectiveness of the shape soon became apparent; hence it was changed to a cylindro-conoidal form, with a nearly hemispherical cup.

In 1855 the Enfield rifle superseded the Minié.   It had three grooves, equi-distant, and one turn in 6 ft. 6 in.; bore ·577.   The grooves, which were at first of uniform depth, were made progressive in 1858, being ·015 inches at the breech and ·005 inches at the muzzle.

In 1866, Lord de Grey, then Secretary of State for War, gave orders for the conversion of a considerable number of the Enfield rifles into breech-loaders on the "Snider" principle.   At first the shooting was not satisfactory, owing to the ammunition being faulty; this, however, was rectified by Colonel Boxer.   The shooting of the rifle is too well known to need further comment.

The "Snider," in its turn, has given place partially to the Martini-Henry, which let us earnestly hope, will speedily be superseded by a more modern breech-loader, the power and accuracy of which has manifested itself on several occasions in the "Duke of Cambridge's" competition at Wimbledon.

Breech-loaders.— Though it is but within the last ten or twelve years that the armies of Europe have been supplied with breech-loading rifles, the invention is by no means modern.   More than *three hundred* years ago this system of loading fire-arms was understood, as is proved by the following extract from Hewitt's *Ancient Armour and Weapons in Europe* :—

"Two examples of the breech-loading arm, both of which appear to have belonged to King Henry VIII, are in the Tower collection.   One of these, No. $^{12}/_1$ of the catalogue, has the royal initials, H. R., and a rose crowned, supported by lions, chased on the barrel, where also is the date 1537.   The other $^{12}/_3$, has the rose and fleur-de-lis carved on the stock, and it is remarkable that the movable chamber which carries the cartridge has exactly the form of that in vogue at the present day."

The progress in small arms was but slight until the middle of the present century, both as regarded the precision of the weapon, and the rapidity with which it could be loaded and discharged; however, within the last quarter of a century, the strides towards perfection have been marked and rapid, as if to atone for the non-inventive genius of our forefathers.

Gunpowder.— To enumerate the details of manufacture would probably weary the reader; it will therefore suffice only to mention a few interesting records regarding the properties of the gases, etc., generated on the ignition of the charge.

Greater differences will generally be found to exist in charges of powder when *measured* than when *weighed.*   The experiments conducted by Robins prove that the weight of the gas generated was three-tenths of the *weight of the powder.*

The pressure of the volume of the gas has been estimated at different quantities by different writers.   Robins assumed it to be at least 15,000 lbs. per square inch;   Dr. Hutton computed it to be about as much again, or 30,000 lbs. per square inch;   others, including Colonel Boxer, computed it to be about 22,000 lbs. on the square inch.

To comprehend fully the process by which the bullet is expelled from the barrel, it is necessary to investigate, as far as possible, the conditions under which the charge of powder is fired.   Assume the space in the rifle occupied by the charge of powder to be, say, one inch.   On ignition this volume increases 250 times multiplied by 6 (increase due to heat of the chemical action), or 1500 atmospheres, *i.e.* 22,500 lbs. per square inch. During the first moment of ignition the pressure rapidly increases from nothing to its greatest amount, and again diminishes as its volume is increased by the passage of the bullet along the bore.

Heat acts in a very marked manner upon gunpowder, as is proved by the following record :— One ounce of powder fired in a 4½ inch mortar, with a shell weighing 8 lbs., gave an average range of 144 yards, but when heated up to 400° Fahr. 242 yards !

The actual velocity of the expansion of the gas cannot be ascertained with absolute certainty. Robins estimated the velocity of expansion at the muzzle to be 7000 feet per second.

Lest some inventive mind might be fired with the desire to improve upon existing principles, as adopted in the construction of small-arms and projectiles, the writer would warn such persons to pause and consider ere they plunge headlong *in medias res*. The Patent Office already contains some very remarkable records regarding so-called improvements in projectiles. The inventors, apparently, have no sooner been struck with the *idea*, than they have rushed off to protect the same by registering it in the Patent Office; seemingly quite indifferent to the fact whether such improvement, or rather *idea* of an improvement, had already been patented.

The impetuous man, who thus hastens to protect his notion of an improvement, not only, too often, wastes his substance, but leaves to posterity a lasting record of his weakness of mind in believing the "impossible" to be a discovery — proves himself, moreover, to have been guilty of the negligence of not having ascertained whether the "impossible" had even the merit of being original !

A few extracts from patents for improvements in projectiles have been culled from the Patent Office records, and will serve to illustrate the folly against which the reader is cautioned.

One rampant idea, which would seem to have taken possession of some *half hundred* brains, has been that elongated and other projectiles might be fired from a *smooth*-bore, and, by some exterior appendages, be made to *rotate*, thereby doing away with the necessity of *rifling* ! Several methods for attaining this end have been patented over and over again, each fresh patentee apparently caring little whether his specification had already been recorded by some one else !

The dates of the patents are given to show until how recently such ideas prevailed.

D. S., 14th May, 1859 :

"Spring feathers may be attached to the projectile, which lie in recesses while the projectile is in the barrel, and expand during flight so as to guide the projectile and give it rotation."

W. E. N., 8th October, 1864 :

"Projectiles intended to be fired from smooth-bore guns are to be made with cylindrical chambers formed in the rear of the projectile, and placed at an angle to the plane of the longitudinal axis of the projectile. The inclined chambers are filled with small charges of powder, which when fired, cause the projectile to rotate on its axis, so that it issues from the smooth-bore piece with a rotation similar to that caused by rifling grooves."

T. G., 18th August, 1860 :

"The projectile is made hollow, and of such a size and shape that it may be fitted upon the exterior of the barrel in which the propelling charge is exploded. Rotation may be given to the projectile by rifling its interior of a shape corresponding to the exterior of the discharge barrel."

W. A. L., 19th January, 1861 :

"Projectiles are to be made with conical fronts, cylindrical middle parts, and tapering rears, wings or vanes being attached to the rear to give rotation. A stem projecting from the rear is inserted in a perforated disc or wad. The projectile may be made or iron, pottery, or glass. Hinged wings may be attached to the projectile, which fly open as it passes through the air."

R. W. W., 14th May, 1861 :

"Projectiles are made in the form of discs, rings, and oblate spheroids in order to obtain cycloidal rotation in contra-distinction to helical or rifle rotation. The projectiles are by preference made eccentric, but with the centre of gravity in the equatorial plane. The bore of the gun is made straight, that is, without twist, and of a section corresponding with the transverse section of the projectile, leaving just sufficient room for the projectile to roll in the bore."

In 1717, 15th May, a "portable gun or machine, called a Defence," was patented, and which was intended "for shooting *square* bullets against Turks" and "round bullets against Christians."

The inventor, possibly, intended the annihilation of the Turk, holding him probably then in the same detestation that the more humane do now, but it is to be feared that the goodly intention would have frustrated its own object by the eccentric course of the square bullet !

It would have been exceedingly interesting and instructive, had the inventors furnished diagrams of the results of the shooting throughout the several distances. The natural inference is that, had any shooting been *seriously* attempted, the specifications would have found their way into the waste-paper basket, instead of within the walls of the Patent Office !

PRINTED AND BOUND
BY
ANTONY ROWE LTD.,
BUMPER'S FARM, CHIPPENHAM,
WILTSHIRE. SN14 6LH ENGLAND